Jewish Journeys near Jerusalem

A Tourist's Guide

by

Jay Levinson

John Jay College of Criminal Justice
City University of New York

Also by Dr. Jay Levinson

Jewish Journeys in Jeruslem: A Tourist's Guide, The Key Publishing House Inc., Toronto, 2010.

In memory of Meyer Kaplan
Mentor and friend

First Edition 2013
The Key Publishing House Inc.
Toronto, Canada
Website: www.thekeypublish.com
E-mail: info@thekeypublish.com
ISBN 978-1-926780-44-3
eISBN 978-1-926780-51-1

Edited by Ruth Pepperman

Cover image, Mony Vineyards © Sheina Carlebach Berkowitz
Cover design, Typesetting and Indexing by Panwar Media
Un-credited photos are © Jay Levinson
Photos credited (Sheina) are taken by Sheina Carlebach Berkowitz
Photos credited with © are courtesy of their corresponding site

Printed and bound in USA. This book is printed on paper suitable for recycling and made from fully sustained forest sources.

Published in association and a grant from The Key Research Center (www.thekeyresearch.org). The Key promotes freedom of thought and expression and peaceful coexistence among human societies.

KPH

The Key Publishing House Inc.
www.thekeypublish.com
www.thekeyresearch.org

Table of Contents

Information for Tourists

Background

This book is a sequel to *Jewish Journeys in Jerusalem*. It is meant to cover those locations for which it is more plausible for a tourist to base himself in Jerusalem rather than in Tel Aviv, the Galilee or the Negev. The definition is subjective. There are numerous historical and archeological sites as well as museums. Some of the sites are industrial facilities with no tours for the public; they are listed to give readers a better insight into the quality of Jewish life in these places, so that the city names are not just spots on the map. Other commercial facilities are open to the public, sometimes with on-site retail sales outlets often at discounted prices.

Please note that museum hours and entrance fees are subject to change. It is always recommended to check hours in advance.

Security

When traveling in the West Bank tourists should obey government instructions and exercise common sense. Contrary to many rumors, West Bank travel has had relatively few security incidents when travelers have abided by instructions.

The West Bank is divided administratively into three zones: A, areas under Palestinian control; B, Palestinian areas under Israeli security control; C, areas under total Israeli control.

Israelis are not allowed to enter Area A. Although foreign passport holders are permitted in Area A, this is not recommended, especially for those tourists who can be readily identified as Jewish. Since numerous roadblocks have been removed, attention should be paid to signs indicating entrance to Area A. Persons holding both Israeli and foreign passports are considered Israeli for this purpose.

Caution and better judgment should always be exercised, especially in Area B. There are no formal restrictions on travelers in Area C.

Basically, there is no requirement that private vehicles (including taxis and rental cars) be specially plated for protection. All public and school buses in the West Bank are required to have such protection. Some tourist buses are equipped with protective shields; others are not. If this is a personal concern, the best procedure is to ask before making a reservation. It should be noted that there are two levels of protection: (1) plating against stones and Molotov cocktails, and (2) protection against gunfire.

If anything happens on the West Bank, ranging from a medical emergency, a flat tire, or just running out of gas to much more serious incidents, call *1202 from any mobile telephone or landline. The switchboard will transfer the call as needed.

This information is being provided as a service to the tourist. It should be noted that this writer travels to sites and settlements in Area C without concern (though observing prudent behavior) in a regular non-armored vehicle.

Media

Arutz Sheva radio station started in 1988 with broadcasts from an offshore ship, the *MV Hatzvi*. The station now broadcasts on the Internet from its website which began in 1995. Studios are located in Beit El. Arutz Sheva has the distinction of being one of the first Internet radio stations. Political orientation is religious-Zionist. There are hourly newscasts, and a significant portion of programming is in English.

B'sheva, a newspaper in Hebrew which covers events from a religious perspective, is owned by Arutz Sheva. The newspaper was first issued on July 19, 2002. It is distributed without charge on Thursdays in religious areas in much of Israel. It has been estimated that this newspaper has the fourth-largest circulation in the country.

Koleinu is a religiously-oriented bi-weekly newspaper distributed free of charge from Ramat Beit Shemesh. The newspaper has general Israeli news and is operated by the *5 Towns Jewish Times* of Long Island, NY. It is available at selected locations in the Jerusalem, Tel Aviv, and Netanya areas. For questions call 052-952-7500.

There are numerous local newspapers usually distributed without fee in Greater Jerusalem, however coverage tends to be local news and commercial advertisements (sometimes publicizing sales in home-headquartered stores with little overhead and significant discounts). Beit Shemesh probably has the most with at least four weekly newspapers (one of which is the local edition of a newspaper circulated in Jerusalem, Bnei Braq, and other cities) and two advertising magazines. These tend to be of limited interest to tourists, except for the shopper.

Keeping Kosher

Readers should consult the *Kashrut* Section of *Jewish Journeys in Jerusalem* for general information.

For questions regarding the kashrut supervision of rabbis in Judea & Samaria one can call Rabbi Schapira, head of the Religious Council, Telephone: 03-906-6495.

Regarding Gush Etzion, it is best to call the Gush Etzion Religious Council at 02-993-9918. HaRav Abba Shaul gives supervision (*mehadrin*); his mobile telephone number is 050-757-5608. Questions specifically related to Efrat can be directed to the Efrat Religious Council at 02-993-1772 and 02-993-3120.

If there is a kashrut question about a specific establishment, it is always best to contact the *mashgiach* and not the owner of the business.

Wine

This book includes numerous wineries in the Judean Hills, the Hebron Hills and Samaria—all grape growing areas dating back to ancient times. Before sampling a wine one should read the label carefully to determine if it is *mevushal* (cooked) or not, and if it is *otzar beit din* (seventh year). Some wineries have retail purchase and tasting possibilities. One should also ascertain if the kashrut supervision also applies to the tasting room (personnel, food other than wine, etc.). Wine festivals very often are staffed by non-religious personnel, and there is no real control over who touches the open non-*mevushal* bottles.

For the convenience of the reader, modern operating wineries are listed in a separate section of this book.

The boutique wine business is extremely competitive, and it is said that Israel has become the country with the most wineries *per capita*. As some wineries have closed, it is recommended to check first before visiting. Sometimes wineries phasing out operations sell their products at very reasonable prices.

South Along the Dead Sea

Dead Sea

The Dead Sea is the lowest point on earth, 415 meters below sea level. It sits on the Syrian-African Rift, which is part of the explanation for its unique geophysical qualities.

The Dead Sea is renowned for the therapeutic quality of its water, which contains 32 percent minerals and 30 percent salt. Only Lake Asal in Djibouti (Africa) is saltier.

Swimming in the Dead Sea is popular, not only for the novelty of forced floating, but also because of the medicinal value of exposure to the sun and minerals. Separate swimming is available at some of the hotels in Ein Gedi, which also offer *mehadrin* dinner menus.

Note: Entering the Dead Sea with an open cut will cause a strong stinging sensation. If the salt water enters your eyes, place your head back past your shoulders.

Masada *(See color plate 1, p 97)*

History

Reports from the 1963–1965 archeological excavations at Masada brought electrifying news. I waited hours in a queue in New York just to get a glimpse at the initial archeological findings. Masada was not a legend. It was true!

One cannot doubt the authenticity of the artifacts recovered from the mountain-top. The buildings unearthed are real and cannot be dismissed (except for a late-Byzantine church, which can be clearly identified by its Christian architecture and symbols). Now, however, decades after the original sensation has quieted down, perhaps a reevaluation of the findings at Masada is in order.

One should realize that there are two sources for the events that transpired on Masada: (1) Josephus, and (2) archeology. Later written accounts are essentially a repetition or embellishment of Josephus' writings.

Josephus (37–100 CE) as a reliable source is quite problematic to say the very least. Yes, he did live at the time of the Jewish Revolt and the subsequent fall of Masada, however he was anything but an objective and detached historian. Born into a family of Cohanim (priests), he seemed to be quite comfortable with Roman culture. Josephus fought against Romans in the Galilee, but an unusual incident stained his name. Cornered with thirty-nine others in a cave, the group apparently agreed to a suicide pact, yet curiously Josephus was the sole survivor. He then switched loyalties and sided with the Romans (in common parlance a turncoat or traitor). Is his account of a similar mass suicide on Masada to be believed? Perhaps the answer is sealed in the annals of history.

Archeological artifacts cannot be dismissed. More than 1,500 amphorae (jugs with handles to facilitate transport) were found on Masada, suggesting a luxurious lifestyle and a plentiful supply of food fit for a king (Herod, of course). An inscription was also discovered, showing the delivery of wine shipped from Italy for Herod. Order in storage apparently was quite strict, dedicating different storage rooms to specific types of merchandise.

Decorations on the walls of the Northern Palace also testify to an opulent standard of living. The interpretation of many artifacts, however, is subjective and not so straightforward. Amongst the 5,000 coins on Masada were those minted in each of the five years of the Jewish Revolt. How did particularly the later coins, produced when Jerusalem was under siege, make their way to the mountain-top fortress? After all, the final "year" was only from Nisan (start of the minting year) until Tisha B'Av (destruction of the Second Temple) several months later.

Shards with names inscribed on them were uncovered. Were these the names of the last ten survivors before they committed suicide (or killed each other), as archeologists posit?

Who were those who made what was in all probability a valiant stand against the Romans? What was their religious orientation? Some of the items discovered suggest a partial answer. Psalm 150 was recovered exactly in the Masoretic text that we have today, as is the case of fragments from Ezekiel. There are, however, problems. A copy of a scroll discovered at Qumran (Book of Jubilees) was also found, as was a large segment of the Apocryphal Wisdom of Ben Sirah (Ecclesiasticus). There was a synagogue on Masada, however its exact use has been clouded by the passage of centuries. There is also strong indication that tithing for Cohanim was also observed.

A plausible interpretation of this unclear situation is that Masada was not the home of one monolithic faith. Rather, it was a refugee center, accepting Jews of all persuasions, fleeing from the advancing Roman army. This is supported by the reported self-inflicted deaths of the defenders, an act hard to reconcile with Jewish Law. Many of the Herodian storage rooms were converted into residences, apparently to accommodate a rapidly increasing population base. Again, there is no definitive answer.

A visit to Masada is definitely recommended, either by ascent on the Snake Path (only for those physically fit) or by the much easier cable car. If nothing else, the scenic views from the mountain-top are absolutely breathtaking. Prior to ascending Masada a tour of the museum at the foot of the mountain (28 minutes with audio headsets) can give the visitor better perspective, so that he can understand and evaluate the ancient ruins. The movie shown before starting the ascent is well-done from a technical perspective, but it does not contribute to a critical evaluation of what happened centuries ago.

One should allot between two and three hours to a tour on the mountain-top. Summer visits are best done early in the morning before the sun becomes too strong. Wearing a hat with sun-brim is advised.

Up the Snake Path

The Northern Palace

Synagogue

Visitor's Information: Tel: 08-658-4207. Fax: 08-658-4464. Entrance and cable car: NIS56 (adult), NIS31 (child). Entrance only (ascent by the Snake Path): NIS20 (adult), NIS10 (child). Cable cars operate from 0800 until 1600 (winter) or 1700 (summer). The actual site is open during daylight hours. Not Sabbath observant.

Sodom

The exact location of Biblical Sodom is unknown, but "Mount Sodom," along the shore of the southern part of the Dead Sea, has attracted popular attention as a possible site. The mountain is made of halite (rock salt). It has numerous pillars, including one often called "Lot's Wife," because of its fanciful resemblance to a female figurine.

Dead Sea Health Products

In 1985 it was realized that the mud and salt of the Dead Sea could be used beneficially for skin treatment. This is in addition to other Dead Sea resources such as magnesium (Mg), sodium (Na), calcium (Ca), potassium (K) and bromides.

A manufacturing and sales program was initiated in Ein Gedi with production on contract. Reaction was very positive, so a pharmacologist was brought in, the product line was greatly expanded, and the Ahava company was incorporated as a company owned by local kibbutzim. Production in the Mitzpeh Shalom plant overlooking the Dead Sea began in 1988. The company has sales agreements in some thirty different countries.

All products, even when not expressly labeled, are certified Kosher for Passover by Chug Chasam Sofer of Bnei Braq.

If driving southward to Ein Gedi, a quick visit to the Ahava factory can yield a glimpse at the production and packaging line. There is also a four minute movie that explains the mineral content of Dead Sea products. Skin care advice is available without charge.

The Ahava visitors' center is open Sunday–Thursday 0800–1700, Friday 0800–1600. Not Sabbath observant. No admission charge. There is a strong effort to sell products.

Ahava is only one of several companies, both in Israel and Jordan, marketing Dead Sea products, ranging from soap, to shampoo, to mud. There are significant differences in the prices of many of these products. Price-conscious consumers should ascertain that if they are paying a higher price, it should be for the quality of the product and not to cover an advertising budget or for elegant packaging (unless the purchase is for a gift).

For the record, Vitalité started as a general cleaning products concern in the 1980s. The company soon found that it could not compete on the export market with large multi-national companies. Vitalité focused its marketing on private label, then added the Dead Sea line in 2000, both under its own name and private label.

For tourists also traveling to Jordan, those Dead Sea products made in the Hashemite Kingdom are not available in Israel for customs tax reasons. They can be brought to Israel as personal baggage in non-commercial quantities. Jordanian prices tend to be less expensive.

How can you buy Dead Sea products and be assured that you are making a good purchase? Many of the mineral soaps are similar. After checking ingredients, a price comparison is always in order. Mud soap poses a different question. One manufacturer refines mud that allows a 25 percent concentration in soap; another enables only a 12 percent concentration.

Another word of advice is also appropriate. There are some companies that purport to sell Dead Sea products. These even include a company in France that imports Jordanian Dead Sea raw materials and another in Bulgaria. All claims should be carefully examined and verified before making a serious purchase.

Ein Gedi

At different times in history Ein Gedi has been inhabited by various peoples. The Roman ruler, Justinian (483–565 CE), for example, destroyed a Jewish settlement there. The synagogue mosaic described below is evidence of Jewish presence. Evidence also suggests Bedouin use of the area from time to time. In 1848 William Francis Lynch (1801–1865), a U.S. Navy officer, "re-discovered" Ein Gedi as part of his expedition on the Jordan River and Dead Sea, but nothing was built. Lynch's interest was that of a naval officer charting new areas as he was to do later in Africa. (Lynch was subsequently to be a captain in the Confederate Navy.) It was only in 1953 that a Nachal para-military outpost was set up near the oasis as a measure personally decided upon by Prime Minister David Ben Gurion (1886–1973) to protect the nearby border. The outpost was civilianized and a kibbutz was established in 1956.

Until after the Six Day War it was difficult to reach Ein Gedi. To the immediate north along the Dead Sea was the Jordanian border. The sole access was from a road connecting with Beersheva. Only in the late 1960s (after the Six Day War) was the Jordan Valley Road constructed, thus allowing easy travel from Jerusalem and the north. Ein Gedi began to grow, though today the kibbutz remains relatively small with 180 members and roughly 400 other residents. Economically the kibbutz is now a resounding success.

Ein Gal is a kibbutz-owned factory for specialized industrial plastics. More commonly known, however, is the kibbutz hotel (kitchen under rabbinic supervision). There is also a botanical garden with plants not only from Israel, but also from other countries. What makes these gardens unique is the hot desert climate.

The botanical garden is open daily from 0830–1630 except Friday, when it closes at 1430. Entrance is NIS26 for adults and NIS22 for children/senior citizens (free guided tours to hotel guests). Telephone: 08-658-4444.

Archeology

There have been several archeological digs in the Ein Gedi area. The oldest ruins that have been discovered purportedly date to the fourth millennium BCE. A temple dedicated to idol worship and 429 vessels were found on a cliff opposite the Dead Sea, but no remains of a settlement were uncovered. There is, however, evidence of Jewish colonization of Ein Gedi from the seventh century BCE until the middle of the sixth century CE with periodic interruptions.

Water

It is not surprising that people lived in Ein Gedi during ancient times. The Bible (Samuel I 23:29) tells us that King David hid in Ein Gedi. One basic reason is that the Ein Gedi oasis has one rare commodity in the desert—potable water.

The Ein Gedi Mineral Water Company began the bottling of water in 1997. It is jointly owned by Jafora-Tabori (established in 1990) and Kibbutz Ein Gedi. The company bottles and sells mineral water from the springs in the Ein Gedi Nature Reserve.

Antiquities National Park

The Ein Gedi Antiquities National Park (as distinguished from the Nature Reserve) contains a synagogue dating to the Byzantine period (third to sixth century CE). A mosaic floor lists the generations from Adam to Japheth (one of the sons of Noah—see Genesis 5:32 and 9:18), the months of the year and their zodiac equivalent, praise to those who funded the laying of the floor, and a dedication in Aramaic.

One oddity was uncovered—the text of a vow pledging the reader to secrecy about the existence of the settlement. Perhaps this was done for security reasons. An alternative explanation is that a curse was placed upon anyone who would disclose the local secret of extracting balsam resin.

Open: April–September, 0800–1700; October–March, 0800–1600. Not Sabbath observant. For fees see below, Ein Gedi Nature Reserve. Telephone: 08-658-4285, 08-658-4517.

Nature Reserve

The 14,516 dunham Ein Gedi Nature Reserve constitutes the largest oasis in Israel. The Reserve is just west of Route 90, which runs the length of the Dead Sea. Springs feed the oasis during the year—Wadi David (with waterfall) and Wadi Arugot. The Shulamit and Ein Gedi springs are seasonal.

The adjacent Ein Gedi Kibbutz contains an extensive botanical garden containing more than 900 species of plants.

For those looking for an experience in nature, the Reserve has a network of nine scenic hiking trails, including a climb to the 400 meter Ha'etakim Cliff. (Hiking is often restricted or prohibited for safety reasons during the winter rainy season, when there is a possibility of flooding.) The routes range from easy (guided tour available upon prior arrangement) to difficult with notice of departure required as a safety precaution).

Open: April–September: 0800–1700; October–March: 0800–1600. Not Sabbath observant. Combined entrance fee to Ein Gedi Nature Reserve and Antiquities National Park: Adults NIS26, Children NIS14.

Ein Fashkha

Until the late 1960s the road south from Jericho ended at Ein Fashkha, a series of more than 200 fresh water springs on the shores of the Dead Sea, fifteen kilometers south of the ancient city. Today Route 90 connects Ein Fashkha with Ein Gedi and ultimately to Eilat in the south.

During Jordanian rule Ein Fashkha was an undeveloped swimming spot often used by residents of the area. Today the springs are part of a 6.12 square kilometer nature reserve.

The park is divided into two very separate areas: a picnic area and a swimming area. (Unfortunately, there is no separate swimming either at the spring or in the adjacent Dead Sea.) Not connected is the Nature Reserve, which is certainly worth a visit by religiously observant tourists.

Some fifteen different plants grow in the Reserve; all are natural to the area. In addition to the vegetation, the springs and streams provide breathtaking views of untouched nature. There is even a large pool with potable water so clean that one can see fish swimming along the bed.

There are two significant archeological finds within the Nature Reserve. One consists of remnants of a Herodian-era settlement (destroyed after the fall of Jerusalem, rebuilt in part, and finally decimated after the Bar Kochba revolt). It contains a large villa and courtyard, as well as a factory. Archeology does not have all of the answers. The purpose of the factory is not clear. Apparently, it was used to produce either balsam or date wine. Whatever the final product, it seems that it was produced in ritual purity, as suggested by the ritual bath on premises.

All too often we tend to apply modern conditions to ancient reality. Today the Dead Sea is an international border between Israel and Jordan. In ancient times, however, it was a transportation route between settlements on both sides of the waterway. This is attested by the docking wharf found at Ein Fashkha.

The Ein Fashkha Nature Reserve is open 0800–1600. Not Sabbath observant. Entrance fee: Adults NIS23, Children 5–18 NIS12. There are open and closed sections. Visits to the closed section are only with an approved guide (either private or from the Reserve). Tours of 60–90 minutes are available Fridays at 1000 and 1200, or by special arrangement, primarily for groups. Telephone: 02-994-2355. Fax: 02-994-7815.

Qumran

The news in 1947 was thrilling in the scholarly community. Ancient scrolls including large portions of Isaiah had been found in a cave near Qumran, a site just south of Kibbutz Qaliya at the northern end of the Dead Sea.

According to the accepted story, Mohammed Ahmed Al-Hamed, a Bedouin shepherd, pursued a missing sheep, wandered into a cave, and made the first discovery of the scrolls.

The scrolls were brought to an antiquities dealer in Bethlehem, who was afraid he was being offered stolen property. Another less scrupulous dealer probably went to the site, found additional scrolls, and started looking for a buyer.

The Syrian Orthodox Metropolitan, Athanasius Yeshue Samuel (1907–1995) showed interest in acquiring the scrolls, as did Professor Eleazer Lipa Sukenik (1889–1953) of Hebrew University, the father of Yigal Yadin (1917–1984), who eventually succeeded in buying three scrolls.

As time went by, scrolls were discovered in eleven caves. Some scrolls made their way to Jordan. Others were kept in Israel. Those in the Palestine Archeology Museum (now the Rockefeller Museum) in Jerusalem fell into Israeli hands during the 1967 Six Day War.

The ruins at Qumran still pose difficult academic questions. Ritual purity was a key to the esthetic life of the Qumran sect, hence it was not surprising when archeologists discover two *mikvaot* (ritual baths). There was an earthenware factory and an area to produce date wine (with 100,000 pits), but then the puzzle begins.

There is no decisive indication about the religious nature of the historic settlement that was probably founded some two hundred years before the destruction of the Second Temple and conquered by Roman soldiers, who occupied the site until after the Bar Kochba rebellion. The only thing universally agreed upon was that for at least some period of time Qumran was inhabited by 200 Jews at most.

Were scrolls stored in the caves as a "library?" Or were the caves a religious center for solitude? Perhaps the scrolls were hidden for a time in the future when pagan Roman soldiers did not threaten the inhabitants. Most (but not all) scholars suggest that Qumran might have been a center for the Essenes, a breakaway sect from mainstream Judaism that has been acclaimed as a source for early Christianity. Here, as in many other places, history has sealed the answers.

An alternative theory suggests that when Qumran was destroyed, it was inhabited by Jews who were fleeing the Roman devastation of Jerusalem. Archeology, though, does establish one clear fact—similarity of pottery with vessels from Jericho and Masada place Qumran not as an isolated hermetic village, but as part of a Dead Sea/Jordan Valley culture.

For orthodox Jews the heretical scrolls are of no importance. They show a religio-cultural identification which is at best an historical curiosity from an era rampant with religiously unacceptable doctrine. Particularly important, though, is the Isaiah Scroll, the oldest extant biblical scroll. Numerous other Biblical writings were also found, but they are essentially fragments. The Isaiah Scroll exists more or less in its entirety.

The Qumran scroll offers no substantive differences from the Book of Isaiah. There are, though, minor variations from the Masoretic text which we have today. Professor E. Yechezkael Kutscher (1909–1971), a religiously observant philologist, postulates that those differences shed light on the dialect pronunciation of the time and the influences of Mishnaic Hebrew and spoken Aramaic.

Today Qumran is a national park worth visiting by those with strong interest in understanding history. When standing behind the visitors' reception building, it becomes easier to grasp why the Qumran caves went undiscovered for so many centuries.

There is a three-screen seven-minute audio-visual presentation at the entrance to provide visitors with a quick historical overview. It is written and produced from a non-Jewish perspective and can well be skipped. The oversized souvenir shop located at the exit can also be excluded from the tour of Qumran.

The Qumran National Park is off Route 90. Hours: October–March: 0800–1600. April–September: 0800–1700. Not Sabbath observant. Telephone: 02-994-2235. Fee (includes audio-visual presentation): Adults NIS18, children 5–18 NIS8. A discounted price of NIS11.50 applies to certain Israelis only.

Although the site is advertised as handicapped-accessible, this applies only to the reception building and its immediate proximity. Many of the archeological sites are on gravel paths that are difficult to negotiate with a wheelchair.

Jericho

Ancient Ruins

On Nisan 22, today the eighth day of Passover in the Diaspora, Joshua began the circumambulation of the walls of Jericho, a city 250 meters below sea level. Then, on Nisan 28, 2489, the walls with their fortifications tumbled. Particularly in the past century archeologists have tried to learn more about the ancient city that succumbed by miracle.

In 1907 two German orientalists and archeologists, Ernst Sellin (1867–1946) and Carl Watzinger (1877–1948), enthusiastically started digging up the ancient city of Jericho, but zeal outpaced careful documentation. The records they kept were lacking, and little was learnt. When John Garstang (1876–1956) directed excavations beginning in 1927, archeology was still relatively new, and methods were again quite primitive. Kathleen Kenyon (1906–1978) excavated the area in the 1950s, asserting 23 different layers of settlement. Unfortunately, early excavations of Jericho were not professional in modern terms. Visiting the site leaves less to see and more to imagine.

In the 1950s all that was found in Jericho was carted away, except for small segments of a staircase and a wall. When one views the *tel* (today located in the Palestinian Authority), he must have a strong imagination to envision that a city once stood there. Oddly enough, it is in the Jordanian National Museum that many artifacts from Jericho can be seen. Jordan ruled Jericho when Kenyon excavated the site, and as a consequence many items were transferred to Amman.

Jericho was a center of idol worship from the beginning of its history. One of the items on display in Amman is an early human head, assessed by archeologists to be the object of some sort of pagan worship.

Trephining was an ancient medical procedure involving the drilling of holes into the skull of a sick person. On display is an historic example of the procedure estimated to be from the Early Bronze Age (before 1900 BCE). The patient survived the first trephining operation, as evidenced by a hole that had healed on his cranium. The second operation apparently was not as successful.

Numerous items from the Middle Bronze Age give a feeling of life in Jericho before the Hyksos invasion. There is a bronze belt fastener apparently belonging to the chief warrior, and an ostrich egg, probably placed in a tomb. The pottery of the era is much improved compared to earlier vessels; the difference evidently was the introduction of a fast potter's wheel. Items on display include one jug in the shape of a bird and another in the shape of a woman.

Late Bronze Age and Iron Age artifacts show very clearly that Jericho shared cultural influences with other contemporaneous cities such as Pella and Amman. This includes white ware and red/brown decorative lines.

Alabaster artifacts were found in the excavations at Jericho. Alabaster is not local, and was probably introduced from Egypt during the Hyksos occupation of the area.

Nothing after about 1200–1100 BCE has been recovered from Jericho. Destruction of the city by Joshua was complete. The ancient city was never resettled, though there were people who lived in adjacent areas. This follows a common practice that it is easier to settle nearby, rather than clear stones from destruction.

In 1952 an early-period tower measuring about 8.5 meters (unusually high for the period) was found at the edge of the ancient city. It is thought that the tower was somehow related to the summer solstice and the casting of shadows over the city.

At the time of writing, a visit to the archeological site in Jericho (Palestinian Authority) is not recommended for security reasons, even for those carrying non-Israeli passports.

The Jordan National Museum due to open in downtown Amman contains material and artifacts about Jericho. Exhibits will have explanations in Arabic and English.

Hisham's Palace

Hisham's Palace, built during the Ummayad Empire, is not a Jewish site, but it gives an instructive glimpse into governmental rule and values in the Land of Israel during the eighth century. The palace is situated on sixty hectares in Khirbat Al Mafjar, west of the Jordan Valley and 260 meters below sea level.

The palace was first discovered in 1873, but archeological excavations began only in 1935 under the direction of Dr. Dimitri C. Baramki (1909–1984). More diggings were conducted there again in 1948 with the efforts of Robert W. Hamilton, a British archaeologist. During the excavations many of the findings were transferred to the Palestine Archeology Museum. Hamdan Taha was responsible for later digging in the 1990s and 2000s.

The winter palace is an excellent example of early Islamic architecture it contains several residential floors, a courtyard with a portico, a mosque, a fountain and a sauna modeled on Roman baths. For many years the site was believed to have been built during the reign of Ummayad Caliph Hisham Ben Abdul Malik, between 724 and 743 CE, but experts now believe his nephew and successor Al-Walid II built the palace and lived in the uncompleted structure. Construction was never completed. An earthquake destroyed much of the palace in 749.

Shalom Al Yisrael Synagogue
(See color plate 2, p 97)

In 1936 Dimitri Baramki, while working for the Palestine Mandate Antiquities Authority, found the Shalom Al Yisrael Synagogue. The basic highlight is a mosaic floor measuring 10 x 13 meters. It was typical of a synagogue floor of the time, with a depiction of a Torah Ark, a candelabrum, a shofar, a lulav, and a Hebrew inscription, *"Shalom Al Yisrael,"* (Peace upon Israel).

Baramki was a Palestinian-born archeologist. After Israel independence in 1948, he moved to Lebanon, where he enjoyed a distinguished career in the archeology department of the American University of Beirut.

The mosaic that Baramki unearthed is judged to have belonged to a synagogue from the late Byzantine period (probably the sixth century CE), although some archeologists date it earlier; as in many other finds, there are no animal or human representations.

During Jordanian rule in Jericho these Byzantine remains were inside a refugee camp on the road from Tel Jericho to Hisham's Palace, and were more or less neglected. In the 1970s Israel demolished the camp, and the Shalom Al Yisrael Synagogue became a point of Jewish tourism. Unexpectedly, an enterprising Arab built a house over the Byzantine floor and requested that visitors pay an admission fee to see the mosaic. As a solution, in 1986 the Israel National Parks Authority purchased the building. After the beginning of the Second Intifada, Jews no longer visit the site without special arrangements.

Na'aran Synagogue *(See color plate 3, p 98)*

The Na'aran synagogue mosaic, unearthed in 1918, is far less complete and probably dates to the Byzantine period. It contains a zodiac motif; visible is the section dealing with Cancer. There is also part of the mosaic on display in the Good Samaritan Inn Mosaic Museum on the Jericho Road.

The village of Na'aran was known from Biblical times, when it was located in Ephraim, on the road from Beit El to Jericho, just north of the latter. The road, still in existence, provides breath-taking views, but it is extremely dangerous with a narrow pavement and (as of last notice) a lack of safety rails to prevent cars from tumbling off the road.

Some 200 meters from the synagogue mosaic is Ein Di'uk, a fresh water spring now used as a swimming pool.

Today both synagogue mosaics are under the control of the Palestinian Authority. There have been reports of damage and repair to the new building at Shalom Al Yisrael. In any event visits to the two sites are not recommended for security reasons. An even older synagogue is located in Palestinian territory near Wadi Qelt; access is also not recommended.

Central Road South

Beitar Illit *(See color plates 4 & 5, p 98)*

Beitar Illit, affectionately nicknamed by residents as Israel's *Heimische Home*, is a flourishing city just outside the Green Line, off the main highway, on Route 375 leading from south of Jerusalem to Beit Shemesh. A unique feature of the city is that all of its more than 40,000 residents are ultra-orthodox. As Eliyah Naeh, the city spokesman points out, the population is not merely Sabbath observant. For all of the locals Torah is a way of life. The city, now situated on 4.3 square kilometers of land, started with only a few families, who had called the settlement of caravans "Hadar Beitar."

The story of Beitar Illit begins with Joseph Rosenberg, who was impressed by the history of Bar Kochba and petitioned the newly elected Likud government of the late 1970s to establish a settlement in the area. Approval was granted for a settlement with a religious flavor, and in 1985 former students of Machon Meir Yeshiva, including Rabbi Reuven Hass (later of Beit El) moved into the aforementioned "Hadar Beitar." The settlement remained very small until a new government decision was reached in the late 1980s. There was a severe housing shortage in the ultra-orthodox sector. The settlement was renamed "Beitar Illit," and ultra-orthodox families were encouraged to take up residence. Hadar Beitar was on high ground above the not-too-far-away ruins of ancient Beitar (see below), hence the new name.

Soon the new families came to dominate life in the settlement and transform it into a large Torah center with dozens of synagogues, schools, and *mikvaot*. Growth was so fast that by 2002 Beitar Illit was officially approved for city status. The original inhabitants, encouraged by a yeshiva in Hebron, decided to relocate elsewhere (some to caravans in a new and very small *yishuv* near Beitar Illit and again called Hadar Beitar).

Beitar Illit is primarily a residential area. There are no museums. There are no hotels. An industrial center is still not complete. In the late 1990s caves were discovered with ancient pottery, but they have not been developed for tourism, and there is little to see. Yet, Beitar Illit is a very pleasant place to visit.

One important attraction is the *Aron Kodesh* (Torah Ark) in the Karlin-Stolin synagogue in the Etrog neighborhood. The massive Ark, built at the cost of about $87,000), is definitely worth seeing. Scenes of the Land of Israel are carved into the façade by hand.

Another synagogue to see is Boyan on Rechov Nedvorna, built on the model of the synagogue in the Ukraine of the Pachad Yitzchak (HaRav Yitzchok Friedman, [1850–1917], the son of HaRav Avraham Yaakov Friedman [1819–1883] of Sadigura, who in turn was the son of HaRav Yisrael Friedman [1797–1851] of Ruzhin).

If you are looking for a break in tourism and a place with large parks for children to play in a religious atmosphere, Beitar is certainly an excellent choice. There is no shortage of grocery stores, supermarkets, and quick food restaurants with appropriate rabbinic supervision to find something to eat.

No, Beitar Illit is not Jerusalem, nor is it Bnei Braq, each with both religious and secular neighborhoods. Beitar Illit is a clean and quiet city developing as a Torah center where synagogues and *yeshivot* form the tenor of life.

Ancient Beitar

Tel Beitar is located a couple of kilometers from Beitar Illit near the old Roman road from Jerusalem to Gaza. The ancient city is surrounded by deep valleys on all sides except the southern side, which must have been the entrance to the city. It is best known as a center for Torah study and for its conquest by the Romans with the killing of Bar Kochba, thus ending the Second Revolt (135 CE).

There have been excavations of ancient Beitar, however only remnants of a city wall and tower have been found. The site is not at all developed for tourism, and it is also off the main highway and through an Arab village. A visit is not recommended for security reasons.

Beit Lechem (Bethlehem)

Beit Lechem is the city where David was crowned as king. The city was sacked by the Samaritans in 529 CE, but it was then rebuilt by the Byzantines. Over the years control of the city has changed hands several times. It is now in the Palestinian Authority except for Rachel's Tomb.

Rachel's Tomb (Kever Rachel)

For centuries Jews have streamed to Rachel's Tomb, "…on the way to Efrat, in Bethlehem "(Genesis 35:19), to offer their prayers. In modern terms Rachel's Tomb is located at the end of a short strip of Israeli-controlled territory less than a kilometer past the inspection point near Gilo.

Rachel the Matriarch is buried in a deep cave. The buildings over the cave are relatively modern and have no particular religious significance.

Travelers mention the site as early as the fourth century CE. At some point a pyramid was erected over the grave, but in 1615 Mohammad Pasha of Jerusalem ordered the pyramid removed and replaced by a cupola supported by four arches. That was reconstructed and strengthened in the eighteenth century. In the nineteenth century Moses Montefiore (1784–1885) commissioned the building of a prayer area adjacent to the arched structure; he had a special affection for the grave, and earth from the site was interred with him according to instructions that he left.

Wells were dug in the compound in the mid-nineteenth century to provide water for travelers.

After the outbreak of security problems and the Al-Aqsa (Second) Intifada, the IDF erected protective walls along the perimeter of the area.

Not only Jews consider Rachel's Tomb as holy. Therefore, Moslems (primarily Bedouin, but also some residents of the area) are buried in a cemetery on surrounding grounds.

For many years Rabbi Tzvi Hirsch Kalisher (1795–1874) and later his son tried to establish a Jewish settlement near the grave, but the effort eventually became impractical with the onset of the Israel War of Independence and the fall of the Rachel's Tomb to the Arab Legion.

Jews have never yielded in their desire to pray at Rachel's Tomb. "Yosef," a religious Jew from Jerusalem who preferred anonymity traveled there every day for more than fifteen years until he passed away. At times it meant "disappearing" from work for an hour. In 2001 the *yahrzeit* of Rachel fell on a Saturday night. At the time there was constant Arab gunfire against Jews trying to visit the grave, and at times access was prohibited by Israeli security forces. How could it be not to visit Rachel's Tomb particularly on the *yahrzeit*? That was unthinkable! Together with a *minyan* of other regulars, "Yosef" and some of his friends traveled to Rachel's Tomb under IDF protection during a lull in the shooting on Friday afternoon. The group enjoyed a unique Shabbat, protected by Rachel the Matriarch as their prayers and sleep were both interrupted by shooting from Arab Bethlehem and Beit Jala. Mission Accomplished. They were there after Shabbat on the *yahrzeit.*

The *yahrzeit* of Rachel falls on Heshvan 11. Every year thousands come to Rachel's Tomb, even in years with heightened political instability. May the prayers they offer be answered!

The road forks several meters south of Rachel's Tomb. To the left is Bethlehem. To the right is the road leading to the Etzion Bloc and Hebron. Today the area is off-limits to the prudent traveler. In former days one could visit a house at the fork, where in the backyard one sees remains of the second century CE Roman water aqueduct leading to Jerusalem. (This is the later of two Roman aqueducts leading from Solomon's Pools to Jerusalem. Parts of the earlier water system were used into the twentieth century. See below.)

Buses to Rachel's Tomb are available from the Jerusalem Central Bus Station on a daily basis and on selected days from near Kikar Shabbat in the Geula neighborhood. Ample parking is available for those coming by private vehicle.

Solomon's Pools

Jerusalem was a dynamic city during the period of the Second Temple. The city grew significantly, particularly in the last century or so before the Destruction. New neighborhoods were added in the Upper City; the population burgeoned; and, there was an increased need for water. The waters of Gihon and locals wells were no longer sufficient to service the city. The answer to the problem was a series of aqueducts, some of which actually remained in use for almost two thousand years!

Five water sources were found in the Hebron Hills, and at various times during the period three aqueducts were built to Solomon's Pools, a series of three reservoirs south of Bethlehem. Two of the pools are ancient, probably dating to sometime between the Hasmoneans and Herod; the third (lowest) pool was added in the fifteenth century during Mamluk rule in Jerusalem.

The aqueducts were an architectural marvel of their time. One covered "only" ten kilometers, but it took forty kilometers of construction winding through the Judean topography to bring water to the reservoirs by the force of gravity. Three reservoirs collecting water that was eventually released to Jerusalem through a meandering aqueduct are located four kilometers south of Bethlehem.

The next challenge was to get the water from the reservoirs at Solomon's Pools to Jerusalem. The Pools are at 760 meters above sea level, and Jerusalem is at 735 meters, so an aqueduct was built to carry water 20.6 kilometers. When they were in full use, the pools held some one hundred and fifty thousand cubic meters (over thirty-five million US gallons) of water.

There were, however, two major problems. The hills in one area of Bethlehem and in the Jerusalem neighborhood of Armon HaNatziv (Arabic, Jebel Mukabir) did not conveniently allow downward flow of water. Circumventing the hills would have been too difficult. It would have meant constructing at least 3.5 additional kilometers of aqueducts. The solution was to build tunnels through the mountains to accommodate the water flow.

After the last tunnel the water flowed to Jerusalem, passing through today's Jewish Quarter (near the parking lot), then to the Temple Mount via what is commonly called Wilson's Arch (named after the surveyor, Charles Wilson (1836–1905), who discovered it in the late nineteenth century).

Following the Destruction of the Second Temple there was no point in bringing water to the Temple Mount, which lay desolate. It seems that the water system was altered, and the final terminus of the aqueduct was in the Upper City.

It must be remembered that although the Romans destroyed Jewish Jerusalem, they were insistent on populating their new city, Alia Capitolina. Again, they needed water. The first aqueduct was insufficient. Probably soon after the Destruction (based upon an inscription that has been unearthed), a second aqueduct was built at a slightly higher elevation than the first (hence it is called the Upper Aqueduct). It covers the fourteen kilometers from Solomon's Pools to Jerusalem in an almost straight line, paralleling the original Lower Aqueduct only within today's city. But here too there were problems. A more sophisticated tunnel had to be cut through the rocks in the Rachel's Tomb/ Ramat Rachel area.

Nothing lasts forever, particularly as flowing water slowly erodes even the hardest stone. The aqueducts were used right through the Ottoman period, but then repairs were needed. During early Ottoman rule, earthenware tubing was inlaid into parts of the aqueducts.

As the Ottoman Empire faltered, so did the aqueducts. Iron pipes were added in 1901, but the system deterioration was too extensive. In 1907 the two-thousand-year-old aqueducts were finally abandoned. There was no reason to make basic repairs. The technology of pumping water had made the aqueducts obsolete.

The best place in the city of Jerusalem to see the aqueducts is Armon HaNatziv, which can be easily reached by car or bus. The tunneling for the aqueduct is part of a playground and recreation area just to the south of the Tayyelet (Promenade). (Next to the tunnel there is an ancient water cistern, which possibly explains why the aqueduct was routed here rather than adding the 3.5 kilometers of construction mentioned above.)

In the field north of the Armon HaNatziv Promenade and slightly to the west there is a segment of the original aqueduct.

An Ottoman fortress built in 1617 (now little more than exterior walls) protected the pools, since they were critical for the Jerusalem population. The name "Suleiman (Arabic/Turkish for Solomon) [the Magnificent]" is inscribed on one of the fortress walls, hence the mistaken appellation, "[King] Solomon's Pools."

Today, Solomon's Pools are in the Palestinian Authority. A visit is not recommended for security reasons.

Biyar Underground Aqueduct

The Biyar (Arabic for "well") is to the south of Solomon's Pools and is part of the water network of which the Pools were the hub. From the Biyar, water flowed with the aid of an underground aqueduct constructed in classic Roman style with support pillars and openings every 15 to 20 meters for 2.8 kilometers. Then the water spilled into an open *wadi* and flowed onward to Solomon's Pools. Let there be no doubt—Herod and his construction engineers were anything but novices when it came to building. The route of the aqueduct was chosen not only to maximize on gravity and the flow of water. The four kilometers to Solomon's Pools were covered in only 4.7 kilometers, maximizing upon gravity. The aqueduct also tapped into other water sources along the way, so that for every liter that left the Biyar, two liters spilled into the Pools.

This site was first developed for tourists in about 2001, but proper organization first started in 2008 with qualified guides, and sturdy, electric lighting. Two tourist paths are available. For the adventurous and non-claustrophobic there is the possibility of walking in the underground aqueduct. For others there is the option of descending forty-four steps into the main room of the aqueduct.

To reach the Biyar Aqueduct drive south from Jerusalem through the tunnels. There will be signs for a right turn opposite Efrat. Turn left, proceed under the highway, then turn left again. Telephone: 02-993-5133 (Gush Etzion Field School). Open summer months only, Sunday–Thursday 0900–1700, Fri 0900–1500. Closed Shabbat. Fee: NIS18 for individuals, NIS15 for people in groups. Shoes that can be worn in the water and a flashlight will help. Picnic tables are available without charge.

Efrat(a)

Background

Efrat was founded in 1983, and as of this writing it has grown to number over 8,500 residents. Archeological evidence (primarily burial caves) suggests that part of the area covered by Efrat was settled as early as the Bronze Age (pre-Israelite period).

Kfar Etzion

Museum

A film in the Memorial Center at Kfar Etzion tells the story. In the hills mid-way between Jerusalem and Hebron, along the Path of the Patriarchs, there were several efforts in the first half of the twentieth century to establish a Jewish settlement. In January 1927, the orthodox Jewish group Zikhron David founded a small farming community, "Migdal Eder," but in the 1929 Palestine riots, Migdal Eder was ransacked. Jews then abandoned the settlement.

Shmuel Yosef Holtzman bought the land in the early 1930s and called it Kfar Etzion, a play on his name, the German "holtz" meaning "wood," which translates to "etz" in Hebrew). Jews were forced to leave again in the wake of the 1936 Arab riots. Kfar Etzion was again destroyed. Then, in 1943 yet another group tried, as they started Kibbutz Kfar Etzion.

Their first building is, perhaps, amusing in retrospect. British authorities had arrested the three or four monks living in a German monastery, and interned them in Sharona (a former Templar colony commandeered by British forces after the start of World War II; today the Ministry of Defense and Israel Army headquarters in Tel Aviv) as citizens of an enemy country. The settlers took over the abandoned building.

Motivation was intense. "Torah and working the land" was their motto. They learned Torah. They observed mitzvot, and they began to reap the benefits of their labor.

By 1945 they were joined by more settlers—refugees from Europe—who started the kibbutz Massuot Yitzchak. One of those refugees described his situation very succinctly, "I have survived to mourn for my family.... We believe in full faith that this was all the will of the Al-mighty.... Let us move to the Land of Israel ... to make a new beginning." Then two more settlements opened in the Etzion Bloc. Jewish life was taking hold with more than 400 inhabitants and 2,500 acres of land.

At the beginning of November 1947 all looked promising, and the UN vote for partition on the twenty-ninth of the month only intensified the optimism of the Jews living in the Etzion Bloc.

By December, however, those Jews were digging defense trenches instead of irrigation ditches. Abdul Kader Al-Husseini (1907-1948), a leader of the Arab opposition to Jewish presence, had set up headquarters in Surif, just to the west. The Etzion Bloc was not included in the Jewish portion of Palestine, and al-Husseini's declared objective was to expel its residents.

The word of impending attack came on December 3, 1947. During the ensuing five months skirmishes were periodic. Women and children were evacuated. At a meeting of the men it was decided to remain and fight. The military objective was to prevent Arab troops from using the Jerusalem–Hebron Road.

A date that will never be forgotten in Israeli history is January 16, 1948. Just before midnight a convoy of thirty-eight Jews had set out for the Etzion Bloc from Hartuv. One person sprained his ankle, and two of his companions accompanied him back to the starting base. At daybreak the convoy was spotted between Jaba and Surif. Fierce fighting erupted, and by the end of the day the thirty-five Jews in the convoy were all killed. Many of the bodies were mutilated. Today a kibbutz is named after the convoy; many cities in Israel also have streets named "Lamed Hey" (letters with the numeric value of "35"). (See also the entry for Emek Ha'ela.)

March 27, 1948 was a turning point. The last convoy headed towards Gush Etzion with supplies was attacked in an ambush near today's Neve Daniel, just south of Bethlehem. No more supplies would reach the stranded Jews

By the eve of Israel Independence the battle for Gush Etzion was lost. Those remaining were gathered outside the building where the Memorial Center is now housed. Some of the defeated Jewish prisoners were cruelly murdered in cold blood. As a survivor in the museum film relates, an Arab Legion soldier caught a girl at the opening of a bunker under the building. He pulled the pin on a hand grenade and told her to toss it into the bunker. She refused, knowing there were others hiding in the bunker. The soldier then tossed that grenade and several other grenades. More people died. In all, 151 Jews lost their lives trying to defend Gush Etzion. Numerous others were taken to a POW camp at al-Mafraq in Trans-Jordan.

The multi-media presentation in the museum takes a dramatic turn. The movie stops. The screen is raised. There, with a protective grating to prevent accidents, is the entrance to the bunker!

On the lower floor of the Memorial Center there is an archive with fascinating material. For example, in Tishrei 5710 (1950) Rabbi Shlomo Goren (1917–1994) (then Chief Rabbi of the IDF), an assistant, and a former resident of Kfar Etzion, visited the area following an agreement between Israel and Jordan. There is documentation in the archive. Goren stayed for two days, then he left for Latrun and other battlefields in Jordanian hands. The other two directed a squad of Arab workers for the next week or so. The job was to collect the bodies of the fallen Jews, in fact left by the Jordanians exactly *in situ*. The bodies of those who died in defense towers were still there. Those shot outside today's Memorial Center had not been moved.

The Jordanians cooperated. Arabs who had fought against the Jews gave testimony about what had happened. The bodies were decomposing, and many identifying marks had been lost. The laundry numbers of clothing were recorded. All personal property, including letters to families, was collected. Even pages of *Siddurim* and *Gemarot* were carefully picked up. Then HaRav Shlomo Goren, back in Israel, convened a religious court as the culmination of the process of enabling widows to remarry.

Not all was found in the rubble of battle and destruction. The Torah scrolls of Kfar Etzion were never recovered. In 1995, however, a local Arab did return stolen property through a third party—two candlesticks taken after the fall of Kfar Etzion. They are now on display in the Memorial Center.

On November 25, 1950 the fallen defenders of Gush Etzion were buried in the new cemetery on Mount Herzl. The Arabs razed almost all of the buildings in Kfar Etzion and established a military base. The Jewish history of Gush Etzion was over until 1967, when it was conquered during the Six Day War.

There is a small two-room museum near the Memorial Center. There, the presentation of Kfar Etzion is not at all as effective as in the Memorial Center.

Open: Sunday–Thursday, 0900–1500, Friday 0900–1100. Closed Shabbat. Entrance fee: Adults NIS16, Children NIS13. Access to the Center is not appropriate for handicapped in wheelchairs, even though there is a handicapped bathroom. The film is available in English by prior arrangement. Telephone: 02-993-5160.

Field School

Adjacent to the historical museum is an agricultural museum belonging to the Gush Etzion Field School. The school runs numerous hikes and trips to Jewish sites in the area.

There is also the possibility of private hikes along marked paths. A map, produced in cooperation with the Field School, can be obtained from Gush Etzion Tourism, Telephone: 02-993-3863. The best known route is the Path of the Patriarchs, giving walkers a practical introduction to the Gush.

Gush Etzion Industrial Park

Lavie Winery (Liqueurs)

There is strong competition amongst boutique wineries. The two partners in the Lavie Winery found out about the highly competitive market when they started their business in 2000. One partner came with a background of food technology, and the other was a security professional. Making wine was new to both of them, and they concentrated on Cabernet Sauvignon, more or less an Israeli standard. After two or three years, however, the business took a curious turn, when someone asked if they could produce a chocolate liqueur. The partner with background in food technology had worked for a company producing chocolate specialties, so he was on somewhat familiar ground. By 2005 the Lavie Winery moved into the liqueur business.

Lavie skirted its competition by developing new products, eventually adding new varieties to their best-selling bittersweet chocolate liqueur. Milk chocolate and white chocolate liqueurs (both dairy) were offered as well as a selection of other flavors such as coffee, honey, butterscotch, and cherry.

It is absolutely clear that liqueur regardless of flavor requires kashrut supervision. Dairy liqueur needs to be *chalav Yisrael* for many consumers, and *pareve* has to be reliably certified. Less obvious is that sometimes there are unexpected ingredients. Some companies, for example, use a cognac (grape) base.

From its small offices in the Gush Etzion Industrial Park, the company sends its products to wine and gourmet stores. Don't look for Lavie in the supermarket. The business decision has been made to concentrate on quality, leaving others to compete in the low price market.

Although Lavie has tried to package their liqueurs with impressive labels and bottles, the company realizes that particularly repeat customers make purchases based on taste, not bottling. Many of the stores selling Lavie offer the possibility of tasting before buying.

And, don't search for Lavie wine. The company is concentrating on the liqueur line, which has won Terravino medals. I visited the factory, still officially called a winery, and was offered a generous assortment of liqueurs to sample. Oddly enough, despite officially being a "winery," there was no Lavie wine to be had. Most important to Lavie, though, is that liqueur sales amongst consumers have grown steadily.

In my independent taste evaluation, the chocolate liqueurs (*pareve*, dairy, white/dairy) rated an unqualified "excellent." The butterscotch was not quite as appetizing. It should be remembered, though, that taste is personal and subjective.

The company's liqueur line, except for almond liqueur, is under the *mehadrin* kashrut supervision of HaRav Rubin. All of the Lavie liqueurs have the certification of HaRav Abba Shaul of Gush Etzion. Only the *pareve* liqueurs are certified for Passover by HaRav Shaul; the dairy liqueurs are *chalav Yisrael.* Most of the liqueurs should be consumed within twelve to eighteen months of manufacture (fruit flavors have unlimited shelf life), and no refrigeration is needed even after opening, but the liqueurs should not be exposed to the sun.

Plans for the near future include a visitors' center with tasting room and retail sales center on a second floor in the factory in Efrat.

To reach the Lavie "Winery" travel south from Jerusalem through the tunnels. Turn left at the southern entrance to Efrat. The winery is located in the Gush Etzion Industrial Park (signs to turn right after the left turn to entrance to Efrat). Telephone: 02-993-1238. Visits must be arranged in advance.

Alon Shevut

Yeshiva Har Etzion

Today there are over 450 students from throughout Israel learning in Yeshivat Har Etzion. Their time is divided between Torah study and mandatory army service. The Yeshiva began in Kfar Etzion in December 1967 (Kislev 5728), then moved to Alon Shevut, twenty kilometers south of Jerusalem, in June 1970 (Sivan 5730). Construction of the permanent Beit Midrash began in 1974, with the significant financial assistance from the now-defunct Knesset Kehilat Yisrael Congregation of Newark, New Jersey. The synagogue had been sold due to neighborhood change, and funds along with religious artifacts were donated to the yeshiva. The Beit Midrash of Yeshivat Har Etzion is now dedicated to the defunct American congregation, and in appreciation, a plaque is displayed at the entrance to the Yeshiva. Some of the religious articles transferred from Newark to the Yeshiva are on display in the library.

Also on display are rare books, some of which are from Yemen, Persia, and Algeria, as well as a holiday prayer book that had been confiscated by the Nazis.

Outside the main building there are the remains of a Talmudic era (fourth to fifth century CE) wine press, with Hebrew and English signs describing the wine production process of the period.

Holiday prayerbook in the yeshiva library

Ancient wine press with signs describing the site

Tsomet – Halachic Technology

When you pass through a metal detector on Shabbat is there a halachic problem?

Modern life has brought endless inventions that have become essential parts of our lives. Some "newfangled things" are conveniences that an individual can forgo on Shabbat. Others, for example security devices such as metal detectors, are so intertwined with public needs that society cannot shut them down or turn them off even once a week. Tsomet, an institute in Alon Shevut was established in 1976 to suggest *halachic* solutions to problems that fall into five basic categories:

1) Most work at Tsomet is somehow related to the medical field. Obviously, there are no Sabbath restrictions in trying to save a life. Tsomet, in cooperation with leading rabbis, has proposed solutions for questions that cannot be answered with such black-and-white simplicity.

   A special panel has been developed to allow a sick person to adjust the settings on electrically controlled hospital beds. Tsomet has also developed a call button using gra*ma* (indirect causation, rather than direct action—a *melacha d'rabanan* [rabbinic prohibition]), which many important rabbis permit for a sick person). Hundreds have already been sold to Israeli hospitals and nursing homes. There is a battery-operated wheelchair with unique Sabbath settings. There is even a special hotplate with which hospital staff cannot tamper, so that the patient need not worry about forbidden *bishul* (cooking).

   What is next? There is a growing concern in hospitals that newborns in maternity wards might be given by mistake to women other than their mothers. A modern method of preventing error is transmitters on both mother and child, creating a "positive match" between the two. But, what about Shabbat? Tsomet is working on it. Practical solutions to the question are being field-tested in a leading Israeli hospital.
2) Security is another major concern. Another Tsomet invention is an entrance control mechanism that allows someone to swipe his card and enter a PIN number, all by *gromo,* rather than the usual Torah-prohibited act found in other readers. This has been permitted for heavily restricted areas, such as certain army bases.
3) Not every device permitted under one set of circumstances is universally permitted. Tsomet has tried to work in the tourism area. Sorry, but the same entrance control reader allowed for a security

installation absolutely cannot be used to open a hotel door on Shabbat. There, one still has to find a hotel with old fashioned locks opened by keys. And, watch out in some hotel rooms for sensors that turn off electricity when there is apparently no one in the room. Today there are even devices that send signals each time an item is removed from the mini-bar.

One approach to the Shabbat kitchen in a hotel is to hire a staff of non-Jews. Tsomet, in cooperation with the Technion in Haifa, is looking into other answers, particularly in the kitchen. Again, the same actions of *gromo* permitted for the sick person, cannot be sanctioned for tourists or vacationers.

4) Years ago agriculture was a leading task at Tsomet. Even such luminaries as the Chafetz Chaim (Yisrael Meir Kagan, 1838–1933) and the Chazon Ish (Abraham Yeshaya Karelitz, 1878–1953) wrote extensive responsa on farm-related questions. Today, however, very few Jews are directly involved in tilling the ground or milking cows. The area that gave Tsomet its first major set of tasks is being de-emphasized.
5) Two-thirds of the program at Tsomet deals with technology, but there is work of a less technical nature. At the request of HaRav Bakshi Doron (1941-), Tsomet developed a five hundred hour course of instruction for would-be converts to Judaism. Today that course is an intrinsic part of *Beit Din* (religious court) decisions regarding potential converts. Tsomet also has an annual series of books, *Techumin*, which deal with the practical application of numerous *halachic* issues.

Finally, what about the metal detector at the Western Wall? There are two versions—a gate and a hand-held wand. Both were developed by Tsomet and have settings to bypass turning on the red warning lights on Shabbat. Instead, there is a change in current that alters the vibration of the machine. The change in current has been deemed not to be a *melacha.* (Don't take that as permission to fiddle with a radio on Shabbat, since there are other prohibitions involved.) As of this writing there are three synagogues in Europe that have started using the wand-style metal detectors on Shabbat.

Remember that not every device can be used under all conditions. A person should always consult a *posek* (rabbi giving a rabbinic decision) to ascertain that a Shabbat mechanism is appropriate and permitted for him.

Ha-Erez 3, Alon Shvut. Telephone: 02-993-1442. Tours of Tsomet are available in Hebrew and English with advance notice. One highlight is an excellent display of the *halachic* principle of *gromo.* To get to Tsomet, one can travel by car or take Bus 161 to Alon Shevut. The Institute is just inside the gate.

Rosenberg Winery – See Kosher Wine Guide

Bat Ayn

Hirbit Hillel, a Jewish settlement of the Second Temple era, is at the entrance to Bat Ayn. It was unearthed in 1990, a year after the modern settlement began. Most striking is an ancient *mikva* with separation between those entering and those leaving. Remnants of the *mikva* can be seen just beyond the Bat Ayn guard post. The probable reason for the division is that those leaving after immersion and purification should not come into physical contact with those first coming to the bath. Charred debris suggests destruction during the Bar Kochba Revolt.

Kerem Ferency – See Kosher Wine Guide

Lone Tree Brewery

This micro-brewery was started by two immigrant couples, who progressed from hobby to profession, learned the trade from courses and reading, experimented with different recipes, then started commercial production in Spring 2010.

The Lone Tree Brewery provides an unusual tour and tasting of seven types of beer (all natural and all under the *mehadrin* supervision of HaRav Abba Shaul of Gush Etzion). Supervision certifies amongst other things that all grains are *yashan* even though grown abroad, and there has been *t'vilah* (ritual immersion) for all equipment (not bottles). The beer specialties are English Northern, American Brown, California Steam, Pomegranate Date, Extra Oatmeal, Pale, and India Pale. There are, of course, alternative names publicized by different breweries.

As Susan Levin, the chief brewer, explains, in technical terms this is ale and not beer. The technical difference, however, is less important than the taste of the drink.

Yeast is an important ingredient in making beer. There are numerous kinds of yeast. Examples are:

- Top-fermenting *saccharomyces cerevisiae* produces ale.
- Bottom-fermenting *saccharomyces uvarum* is common in lager-type beers.

Choosing the right yeast (and there are many species) is an art. If you choose *saccharomyces zygo* or *brettanomyces* to make wine, your batch will quickly spoil. *Saccharomyces cerevisiae* is the most frequently used in baking. Confusing? Not really. Levin describes the distinctions and varieties very clearly. For the household, choosing yeast is simplified by commercial labels; for the brewer the right choice is part of the art of making beer.

Another key ingredient in Lone Tree is the grains (usually in combination and relative proportion) used. One type of ale uses a mix of four different species of barley as well as oatmeal, which are all measured with exactness and crushed before the six hour processing begins.

Lone Tree Beer is not easy to find in stores. The micro-brewery is a startup, and only eight hundred to one thousand bottles are produced each month. Sales are divided more-or-less evenly into categories of walk-in customers, restaurants and caterers, and on-shelf sales in Gush Etzion and Jerusalem food stores. Since the beer has no artificial preservatives, recommended storage is no more than about six months. Many commercial beers are heavily laden with preservatives and last much longer. Unlike wine, beer does not improve with aging.

There are preservatives in Lone Tree Beer—hops, which give stability, a slightly bitter taste and also act as a totally natural preservative. For the uninitiated, hops are female flower clusters (strobiles), and come in numerous species, many of which are used for beer. Again, selection is part of the art of a brewer.

Ecology is not forgotten at Lone Tree. Gravity rather than electricity is used to move water. After grains are used and no longer needed to prepare beer, they are served as cereal or donated to the Deer Park (see below) for animal feed.

Tip: Lone Tree Beer is best served when chilled to refrigerator temperature. Cooling to almost freezing suppresses taste and is best for low-quality brews.

Tours are available in Hebrew and English. Between 30 minutes and an hour should be allotted, depending on your level of interest.

Visits can be arranged by calling 050-530-6036 or 054-234-5439. There is a fee for groups. Tasting and beer purchase are possible. The company is expanding and is looking for a larger facility in Gush Etzion.

Coming from Jerusalem, turn right at the Gush Etzion Junction. Proceed towards Bat Ayn, then turn right at a small road just before the Bat Ayn Circle. There is a sign in Hebrew for the deer park; there is no sign for the brewery. Proceed for about two kilometers. The brewery is on the right, just opposite the Deer Park; parking is just before the brewery (not paved).

Note: Boutique or micro-breweries are quite new in Israel, and there are several start-up operations, including some in the geographic area covered by this book. Lone Tree is perhaps one of the better established breweries, even though it is quite new. Not all of the breweries have rabbinical supervision (as noted, Lone Tree does).

Deer Park

Although called the Deer Park, this is much more. It is a rich outdoor experience ranging from a petting zoo to the world's second longest zip line, (a reinforced wire 600 meters long and 120 meters above ground. Those of adventurous spirit can strap themselves into a secure harness and glide down the descent. For those who are less daring, there is arrow shooting, pony riding, and arts and crafts to keep children occupied in a rustic atmosphere.

Coming from Jerusalem, turn right at the Gush Etzion Junction. Proceed towards Bat Ayn, then turn right at a small road just before the Bat Ayn Circle. There is a sign in Hebrew for the park. Proceed for about two kilometers. The park is on the left; parking is on the right (not paved).

Daytime hours are Sunday–Thursday 0930–1730 and Friday 0930–1430 in the summer; for winter hours inquiry must be made. Sabbath observant. Fees vary according to activity, but typically are about NIS40 to NIS45 per person. Telephone: 02-570-9768, 050-204-1201, 050-538-8705. The restaurant is meat and under the *mehadrin* supervision of the Gush Etzion Rabbinate. Query for hours.

Masu'ot Yitzchak

At the approaches to Bat Ayn (coming from the Jerusalem-Hebron Highway turn right before Bat Ayn and follow the signs for about one kilometer) are the remains of Masu'ot Yitzchak, destroyed during the 1948 fighting, as well as the water source that served the settlement.

Remains of the pre-State settlement

Elazar

The modern settlement has a rich ancient past. It began in 1975 as a *moshav* run by ten religious families who had emigrated from North America. The settlement was named for the Elazar, brother of Yehudah the Maccabee who was killed at the Battle of Beit Zechariah in 162 BCE near the community's location. The *moshav* status was dissolved after problems in 1987. It is now home to five hundred families, many of whom are English speaking.

Beit David *(See color plates 6 & 7, p 99)*

Art comes naturally to Meir Yizraeli, born in Jerusalem in 1929 to ultra-Orthodox parents whose families had come to the city in 1851 and 1920 respectively. Meir started in theater, then learned the art of marionette in Italy, not only as a puppeteer, but also as an artisan making puppets from wood. That education in the 1950s changed his life. Although he returned to Israel and was involved in puppet theater, slowly he turned to wood as an art medium. He rejected the secular lifestyle of his colleagues, and concentrated on religious and Israeli artistic subjects. By 1975 he was set in his ways—Judaica art subjects in wood.

Yizraeli's style is to paste small pieces of wood to form his picture. His method is unique and very successful, even though his studio is in two modest and crowded rooms in the yard next to his house. He is very particular in the wood that he uses. During my visit I was shown a tree trunk imported from Spain! This is the raw material that Yizraeli would be using.

As Yizraeli progressed, he opened a gallery on Rechov HaRav Kook in downtown Jerusalem (where the House of Psalms gallery is now located), then he moved to Elazar in 1994.

Not everything is professional in Yizraeli's life. Given his background in theater, he volunteered in religious schools to assist in their student productions. He was also part of the IDF liberation of Gush Etzion in 1967 (part of the reason that he moved to Elazar, and a subject of the frequent lectures that he gives).

The gallery is very much worth visiting. Although the asking price of many of the pictures is quite serious (though a "good buy" for art), there are numerous smaller pictures and items of woodwork that are much easier on the pocketbook. There is also a side room in which Yizraeli has antique Judaica items.

The gallery is located at Rechov Yehudit 69, Elazar. Open during standard business hours, but it is always best to call in advance. Telephone: 02-993-4418. Explanation of artwork in Hebrew, not English. No fee is charged. There are signs in Hebrew directing visitors from the entrance to Elazar.

Herodian

True to his legendary paranoia, Herod built a lavish and heavily fortified palace today known as the Herodian. It is fifteen kilometers south of Jerusalem, and five kilometers south-east of Bethlehem. He spared no effort. He skimped on no luxury. He shunned no expense. But why did he build at the edge of the Judean Desert?

The answer is to be found in Herod's flight from Jerusalem in 37 BCE, after he had served as governor. His rule was challenged, and he was attacked as he retreated. Miraculously, from his point of view, his life was saved in a military victory over his foes. Three years later, after forging new alliances in Rome, he returned to Jerusalem as king, and ordered that a palace be built on the site of his previous victory. Construction was started in 23 BCE, and completed three years later. Workers artificially added height to a low hill, and built the Herodian. The building on the hill served Herod as summer palace, fortress and monument until he died in 4 BCE.

Ruins at Herodian (Sheina)

Ruins at Herodian (Sheina)

Synagogue at Herodian (Sheina)

The palace was the epitome of unabashed pleasure. Round architecture pleased the capricious king's fancy, so the basic building and its four watchtowers were round. The reception area was large, but it was overshadowed by the bath house, which offered cold, lukewarm, and hot pools, with water stored in vast cisterns and heated by a steam system underneath the floor. Water was scarce at the edge of the desert, but that was of no consequence to Herod. Nor were these ordinary baths (at a time when bathing for common folk was a rare privilege). The bath area was a center of lounging and relaxation, where one could divert attention from serious matters for hours.

The commanding height of the edifice made it virtually impregnable, but everything comes to an end. Herod's son, Archelaus, inherited the Herodian, which he kept until 6 CE, when he was banished by the Romans.

The second period in the Herodian's history began in 66 CE, when Jews rebelling against the Romans took over the site. There they turned the reception area into a synagogue, and added a *mikva* to the premises. After the destruction of the Second Temple and the fall of Jerusalem, the rebelling Zealots used the Herodian as one of the three primary places of refuge from the pursuing rulers (in addition to Masada and to Michvar, to be covered in future volumes of this series). But, the Herodian also fell after strong attacks by the Roman army.

The story of the Herodian did not stop there. During the Bar Kochba revolt the Herodian served as a command center and starting point for sneak attack operations—call it guerilla warfare, if you will—against the Romans. An extensive tunneling system from the top of the mountain was dug by Jewish forces, which would use hidden exits to initiate actions against the Romans.

After the Bar Kochba rebellion was defeated, the building went unused and collected dirt over the centuries. The Herodian was well-known from descriptions in Josephus, but it was not until 1962, then again in 1967, that archeologists began excavations under Jordanian direction. It was only after the Israeli excavations that started in 1972 had progressed for several years that the previously unknown Bar Kochba tunnels were discovered.

In recent years there has been speculation that a very elegant grave that has been uncovered might be that of Herod.

Several kilometers away is the hilltop of Asfar, mentioned in the apocryphal I MaccabeeMacabees 9. The site offers an excellent view of the area. It all gives an understanding of the Herodian's strategic value overlooking all approaches, with a clear view of Jerusalem on the horizon.

The only practical way to reach the Herodian is either with an organized tour or by private car. Walking from the nearest bus is absolutely not recommended for security reasons (though the site itself is quite safe). Be prepared for inclines and steps. Hours: 0800–1600. Not

Sabbath observant. Entrance fee: adults NIS22, children (5–18) NIS11. Discounts for seniors are restricted to Israeli citizens. Allot about two hours to your visit.

Tekoa

Tekoa, five miles south of Bethlehem, was established in 1975 as a Nahal outpost. It was civilianized in 1977.

Winery – See Kosher Wine Guide.

Neve Daniel *(See color plates 8 & 9, p 99 & 100)*

There are contradictory trends in the Israeli economy. Particularly in recent years large conglomerates have absorbed smaller companies, if not by outright purchase then by exclusivity contracts. At the same time, however, there has been a trend to start small businesses to target a market void that cannot be filled by mass production. This is perhaps best seen in boutique wineries which have sprung up throughout Israel. Some of these have done well, others have failed, and many struggle on with the hobbyist's dream of ultimate success.

Two of these home-spun start-up companies, both owned by relatively recent immigrants from the United States, have sprung up in Neve Daniel, a Jerusalem suburb. Their products are innovative and promising, and now the owners are working on the hurdle of distribution.

Cookie Crave

The Cookie Crave is a unique home operation run with the idea that cookies can make a very unique gift for the proper occasion.

David Gross is an immigrant from Far Rockaway, New York who made aliyah with his wife in 2004. After trying Har Nof for a short time, he moved to the small town atmosphere of Neve Daniel. With a background in Food and Hotel Management, Gross looked to fit into the job market. After extensive research he came up with an innovative answer—decorative cookies! Instead of bringing a bouquet of flowers as a dinner gift and watching them wilt, a display of cookie "flowers" made from dough can be much more practical. Take your pick from sunflowers, tulips, or an assortment all arranged (even with a "butterfly") artistically in a flower pot or watering can.

A sign reading "Shabbat Shalom," "Mazal Tov," or other message on a cookie-card is optional.

Making *Sheva Brachot?* Gross can supply cookies with the figures of bride and groom replete with their pictures, computer scanned, printed with food coloring and absolutely edible. There are "apples" for Rosh Hashanah and cookie-pops instead of lollipops. The selection is limitless with hearts, smiley faces, business cards, etc. Any shape that you want, Gross will bake it! Orders can be made by phone (02-993-3178) with delivery in much of central Israel possible for large-enough orders. Gross is now working on international shipping, which is already possible by air or express mail for certain products.

Cookie Crave emphasizes cookies, but they do make other pastry items not available in the factory-like production lines of usual bakeries. These include cakes, Danishes, and other delights such as almond or jelly tarts or New York-style black and white cookies (all rated extremely positively by this writer).

All products are *pareve* and *mehadrin* baked in a separate kitchen in the basement of Gross' house. The local Rabbanut is notified before all baking, and a *mashgiach* is invited.

Orders and visits can be arranged by calling telephone: 02-993-3178. United States Telephone (VoIP): 718-360-8625.

Chocoholique

Marc Gottlieb lives just down the street from David Gross, and he, too, has American roots—born in White Plains and having lived in Cedarhurst for a number of years. With backgrounds in the food services industry and computer web design, Gottlieb also sought a place in the Israeli job market.

The beginnings of Chocoholique are worthy of a story book tale. Gottlieb always liked to dabble in food, and one Succot he prepared chocolate liqueur for his holiday guests. Shimona Gotlieb (close in spelling and not a relative) was enchanted with the drink. Soon discussion moved to a business arrangement, and Gottlieb & Gotlieb became Chocoholique.

The first product was Peanut Butter Chocolate Liqueur, made for Purim 5769 (2009). As Marc Gottlieb explains, "There are tried and true food combinations … and this is one of them." Although the combination might initially sound strange, think for a moment about Reese's Cups, marketed by Hershey's.[1] The peanut butter chocolate cups have

[1] The non-Jewish products are mentioned to show general taste acceptance. They are not chalav Yisrael.

sold millions since introduction into the market in 1928. Today Peanut Butter Chocolate Liqueur is Chocoholique's leading seller.

Peppermint Chocolate Liqueur is reminiscent of York Patties. Chocolate Cherry makes one recall cherry pralines. Coconut Chocolate brings to mind Mounds Bars, on the market under different names since 1921. Intense Chocolate is just a higher proportion of chocolate. But what about Chili Pepper Chocolate Liqueur? Oddly enough, that is my favorite. After a sip the first sensation is that of chocolate, then it is enhanced by the chili pepper. The best suggestion is to try it!

There is another factor which makes Chocoholique products different. In many chocolate liqueurs the natural cocoa butter is separated and removed from the cocoa powder, since it does not mix with the water used in the liqueur-making process. Chocoholique uses a natural stabilizer to keep the cocoa butter in the liqueur, thus helping to create a smoother taste. The 7 percent alcohol content is low enough not to overwhelm the taste of chocolate.

To arrange a visit, to place an order, or to find out where products are sold, call Marc Gottlieb at 02-991-9443. *Mehadrin* kashrut supervision by Gush Etzion Rabbinate; all products used are Eida-supervised and *pareve* but not for use on Passover. Shelf life is about six months.

Hebron Area

Halhul

Biblical Graves

Hebron has been a traditional burial area over the centuries. Graves in the vicinity include Gad "The Seer" (I Chronicles 29:29) and Nathan, the Prophet—- today both inside a mosque. Yishai (father of King David) and Osniel ben Q'naz are also buried in the area. Moslem sources also locate the tomb of Jonah in the city.

Although many people mistakenly think that the suburb of Halhul is a purely Arabic name, this is not so. It is mentioned in Joshua 15:58.

The city is in the area controlled by the Palestinian Authority. A visit is not recommended for security reasons.

Hebron

Cave of Machpela

Since ancient days Jews have come to Hebron to pray at the graves of the patriarchs. For many centuries those Jews were allowed only as far as the seventh step. One major exception was the Chesed Abraham (Abraham Israel Pereyra c. 1644–1699), who was allowed as far as the eleventh step. What are these steps? Where were they? What is their meaning for us today? A look at the history of the Cave of Machpela will help supply the answer.

Today there is a mosque that sits over the area, but from archeological evidence it appears that the walled enclosure of a synagogue had been built on the spot sometime during the period of the Second Temple. It is at that time that grave markers were put on the floor of the area above the actual burial level.

There is no question about the authenticity of the location. It has been known since the time of the First Temple. Underneath the building there are two caves, one connecting to the other, hence one of the reasons for the name Machpela (doubled).

In addition to the patriarchs, there are various traditions about others being buried at the spot, outside the confines of the original building.

One tradition says that Adam is interred there. Another tradition says that Esau (or just his head) is buried there.

According to Josephus, the Jewish settlement in Hebron was utterly decimated at the time of the destruction of the Second Temple; that has been confirmed with the finding of appropriate ashes and burn stains at Tel Rumeida (see below), but archeology shows that the Jewish construction over the Cave of Machpela was saved.

The Byzantines made significant changes. The eastern third of the enclosure over the graves was transformed into a church. The remainder of the area was left open. It was in that area that a small synagogue was erected. This has been partially confirmed with the finding of the joining of a roof with the exterior wall. As one would expect, that synagogue faced north—towards Jerusalem.

The Cave of Machpela was changed dramatically after the Arab conquest of Hebron in 637. The Byzantine church was transformed into a mosque, and many of the architectural changes made by the Byzantines were replaced by the Moslems. Yet, Jews were still allowed to pray inside the enclosed area.

In 1099 Christian crusaders re-captured the city. They restored the eastern area of the enclosure to serve as a church and added a fortress, one of the walls of which still stands today. During Christian rule, Jews continued to visit the Cave of Machpela. Benjamin of Tudela, for example, came in 1173. But, Christian rule was not to last long. In the middle of the thirteen century the Mamluks, a fanatic Moslem people, captured Hebron. They constructed buildings in the city (as they did on a much larger scale in Jerusalem), and they replaced all Christian symbols in the Cave of Machpela. They also introduced one change which would last until 1967—Jews (and other non-Moslems) were forbidden to enter the Cave of Machpela enclave. Not only were Jews barred from going into the mosque area, but they were also not allowed anywhere at all within the walled zone. If on occasion a Jew surrupticiously succeeded in entering, public prayer was absolutely out of the question.

After the Mamluks, the Ottomans added sections over the cave, but they made no change in the prohibition for Jews to enter the enclosed zone. That policy was continued under the British Mandate and Jordanian rule.

What, then, was the seventh step where Jews were permitted to pray? Along the outside of the eastern wall there was a staircase that led to an entrance to the enclosed area. It was on those steps that Jews prayed. Those steps were totally outside. Change came in 1967 with Israeli rule over Hebron. Jews were allowed inside the Cave of Machpela enclosure. In the following year the staircase was destroyed. It was a memory too bitter to sustain. It was totally demolished.

What about entering the actual cave itself, and not just the building above it? The entry has been blocked since the Mamluk era, and tradition says that anyone going into the cave will not survive.

A girl was lowered into the cave in 1967 then on the first night of Slichot in 1982 a group of Israelis removed the closure to the cave and entered. In each case all survived.

The actual burial area could not be seen due to fill-in accumulated over the centuries. They did find earthenware vessels apparently from the period of the First Temple. It was clear that Jews had been coming to the Cave of Machpela and to the graves of the Patriarchs for many centuries.

Today the Cave of Machpela is divided into Moslem and Jewish prayer areas. Each religion can pray in the entire building for ten days a year. It is recommended to visit Hebron when there are special events, such as Shabbat of Chaye Sarah (lodgings available) or Chol Hamoed, although a visit is always possible for more quiet prayer (except for the ten "Moslem days").

Avner ben Ner

The grave of Avner ben Ner (I Samuel 14:50, 20:25 and others) is located next to the Cave of Machpela, but it is closed most of the year.

Hebron's Modern Cemetery

A couple of hundred meters from Tel Rumeida is the modern cemetery that serves Kiryat Arba and Hebron. There, the murdered victims of 5689 (1929) are buried. (During Arab control over the cemetery the graves were uprooted, and a shack was made from the tombstones. After the area was taken by Israel in 1967, the cemetery was restored.) One unusual pair of graves are those of HaRav Eliahu Mani (1818–1899) and his wife. Their graves face the Cave of Machpela, and not Jerusalem. He was of the opinion that the Resurrection of the Dead would start with the Patriarchs.

Jewish Buildings in Hebron

Emissaries from the Underground came to Hebron on Av 16, 5689 (1929). There was a threat of a pogrom, and they brought weapons to help the Yishuv defend itself. But, they were turned away by Jews who naively thought their neighbors would never raise a hand against them. The next day Shmuel HaLevi (Wolkowisker) Rozenholtz was murdered in cold blood. Jews in Hebron went to the Mandate Police Station, then in today's Beit Romano, and they were told not to worry. They would be protected. The Mufti in Jerusalem, Hajj Al-Amin Husseini (c. 1895–1974), continued to incite his followers with accusations that Jews were attacking the Temple Mount. For two and a half hours on Shabbat morning Parshat Ekev, Arabs wrecked havoc in Hebron, leaving sixty-seven Jews dead. Jewish survivors were hoarded into Beit Romano "for their protection," then three days later they were transported out of Hebron. The city's centuries-old Jewish population had come to an end.

Since 1968 there has been a concerted effort to renew Jewish presence. On Passover of that year Jewish families spent the holiday in an Arab hotel in Hebron. After the festival they stayed put. They did not leave. That group became the seed of Kiryat Arba and of the Yishuv in Hebron. As of this writing some ninety-three families call the four Jewish neighborhoods in Hebron "home."

The site of Biblical Hebron is now known as Tel Rumeida. Part of the Canaanite city wall can be seen. The width of six meters is clear; archeological estimates are that the wall stood ten meters high. Along the wall there is an original staircase (not restored!) thought by archeologists to be about four thousand years old. Excavations have yielded about forty storage jugs from the time of Abraham, as well as wooden jewelry from about three hundred years later.

Seven jars have been discovered from the period just before Sancheriv (also called Sennacherib; died 681 BCE). Those jars were made to hold grains, and they were labeled to leave no doubt who owned them. They were the "Hebron" property stocks that belonged "*lamelech*" (to the king). Wine cisterns and mosaic floors have been unearthed from the post-Biblical era.

Another highlight of Tel Rumeida is the graves of Ruth and Yishai. The Arabs tried to build a mosque over the graves and claim the territory, but the ruse did not work.

Beit Romano was originally constructed in 1879 by Abraham Romano, a wealthy Jew from Constantinople. After Romano's death the building became the residence and yeshiva of the S'de Chemed (Rabbi Chaim Cheskia Medini, 1833-1904), whose private room has been preserved, though it is unmarked. Eventually, the yeshiva was purchased by Chabad for their use as a center of learning, then it was expropriated by the Mandate Government as a police station. After Jews were chased from the city in 1929, Arabs used the building as Madrasat Usama ibn Munqidh, a school for boys. After the Six Day War the Lubavitcher Rebbe, Menachem Mendel Schneerson (1902-1994), ceded the property (the Arab school and the adjacent land used by Arabs for a bus station) to a representative of the Hebron Jewish Community. Tourists who now visit Beit Romano should not be surprised at what they see—a thriving yeshiva with dormitories.

Beit Hadassah, built in 1893 as a medical facility of the Hadassah organization, today houses ten Jewish families. It also contains a museum (admission free) that tells the story of the Jewish presence in Hebron.

The Slobodka Yeshiva (originally founded in 1881 by Noson Tsevi Finkel (1849-1907) in Slobodka, a suburb of Kovno) moved into Hebron following anti-Semitic acts in Europe. The Jewish population of the city soon grew to 1,500. Four years later, after the riots of 1929, the yeshiva again moved, this time to Jerusalem. Many of the students who remained in Europe at the Slobodka Yeshiva were murdered during the Holocaust.

Another area that has been rebuilt is the Avraham Avinu neighborhood behind what used to be the Arab *suk*, or "marketplace." This was the primary Jewish area of the sixteenth and seventeenth centuries. It was started in 1540 by Jews who had fled the Spanish Inquisition, and one of the first edifices constructed was, of course, a synagogue.

As local lore relates, in 1619 a plague hit Hebron, and many of the residents fled. On Erev Yom Kippur only a *minyan* of Jews remained. One of those ten took ill and sought medical care in Jerusalem. He promised to return before Yom Tov, but as the hour became closer to the time of Kol Nidre, he was not to be found. Unannounced, an old man showed up in synagogue and completed the prayer quorum. One of the synagogue members invited him home after the fast, so that he could break the fast, but he excused himself to straighten up and never came to dinner. The would-be host waited for his guest, then fell asleep. In a dream the mysterious guest identified himself—Avraham Avinu. And so, the name of the neighborhood.

A guided tour of the Yishuv in Hebron is recommended, although tourists can wander by themselves from site to site. The area can be reached safely by Egged or special tourist buses. The former Slobodka Yeshiva in Hebron is in the Arab-controlled part of the city and cannot be visited; that yeshiva was transplanted to Jerusalem, where it became known as the Hebron Yeshiva.

Tours in English, run by the Hebron Community can be arranged by calling 052-431-7055.

Kiryat Arba

Kiryat Arba, founded after the Six Day War in the compound of the military governor and now a thriving town of 7,500 residents, lies just outside Hebron. Although most tourists drive through Kiryat

Arba on escorted tours taking them elsewhere, a visit to the town is certainly worthwhile.

Museum

The Eretz Yehudah (Judea) Archeological Museum was opened in 2003 on the third floor of the municipality building. There the history of the Hebron Mountains can be seen from the artifacts on display.

At the entrance to the museum there is a Herodian-era ceramic from the floor of a public bath. Ceramics in the area from Jerusalem to Hebron were different from those in the rest of the country during this period. Designs were without the usually found human and animal figures. This was due to religious sensitivities.

The museum is arranged in chronological order. Life in Hebron starts before the period of Abraham. Even then the city was inside a wall (hence Purim is celebrated on the fifteenth day of Adar). Numerous handmade pitchers used in idol worship have been retrieved and are on display.

From 2200 until 2000 BCE, just before Abraham, there was a significant change. Tools were introduced to improve the quality of pottery, but vessels were no longer found in buildings; they were put into graves for the deceased to use during the after-life. This belief in a material world after death remained. Even one thousand years later graves contained extensive collections of pottery. Perhaps part of the reason was the rule of the Hyksos and Egyptians in the area.

Eretz Yisrael was part of international trade. The museum contains a Late Bronze Age artifact apparently made in Cyprus as well as Greek-influence items.

What was the area like during the period of Joshua and the Judges? Archeology and the artifacts in the museum provide no clear answer. Canaanite influence in some of the items discovered does hint that there was cultural interaction and not a period of total war without respite.

In the period of the First Temple most Jews were buried in family plots. Drinking vessels have been recovered from some burial areas, but their use was very different from that of the pagans. Those earthenware vessels were apparently used by visitors who came to visit graves.

Two items from the period of the Second Temple are of particular interest. One is part of an ossuary that contains the word "*Yisrael*." The other is a set of stone vessels. Although they are not particularly artistic, they have the advantage of not being *meqabel tum'a* (receive ritual impurity).

The museum is open mornings with tours in English or Hebrew. Prior arrangements are required. Call 02-960-5526. Closed Shabbat. Fee: NIS15.

Winery – See Kosher Wine Guide

Technology

Have an innovative technological idea related to ecology? Mofet, one of the 23 technology "incubation" centers in Israel, provides funding and working space to develop theoretical ideas into marketplace products. Some of the products in Mofet are a computer program to assist people who stutter, a membrane bio-reactor to filter water, and a sun battery for use in colder European areas. (Tours of the facility can be arranged though the Mofet office. Telephone: 02-996-3880.)

Maale Hever (Pnei Hever)

This small settlement is in the eastern Hebron hills in the municipal jurisdiction of the Har Hebron Regional Council. More than fifty families live there. Ma'ale Hever started as Nahal Yakin on January 31, 1983 as a Nahal outpost. It was civilianized on August 24, 1983.

Holy Cacao

Even in a short conversation, Jo Zander's enthusiasm for chocolate is contagious. Zander, a former resident of Northern New Jersey, has realized his dream. Chocolate is now both his hobby and his career. There is, however, a parallel story. As Zander's love of chocolate grew, he also became a *baal teshuva.*

Zander takes pride in the fact that he is the offspring of three generations of bakers, and after an unhappy try at an electrical engineering program, he thought that he would follow the family tradition. In 2002 he enrolled at Johnson & Wales University in Denver in their culinary and pastry track. There was a basic problem. As a *baal teshuva* he quickly realized that in cooking classes he could not cope with the prohibition of mixing milk and meat. He opted for pastry courses.

At the end of the academic program Zander was obligated to take a four month internship. Influenced by a German teacher of chocolate manufacture, he moved with Devorah Grazi, his newly-wed wife who also adopted Orthodox Jewish practice, to Bad Gotesburg, a suburb of

Making chocolate ©

Bonn, and apprenticed in a pastry shop. He baked the typical cookies and cakes, but every week or so he was tasked with making thousands of candies—chocolate candies. "This was a great experience for me," Zander recalls. The apprentice worker resisted temptation. For four months he tasted none of his pastry and candy creations, since they were made on non-kosher equipment.

Israel was the stop after Germany, and for two years Zander learned in yeshiva in Meitzad (Asfar), a small settlement at the southern end of Gush Etzion. Then he was employed as a chef, but he could not shake the bug of chocolate. The influence was Steve DeVries, an icon in the chocolate business, who "wouldn't use any beans that he wasn't present for the harvesting and the fermenting and the drying…" DeVries started the American trend of small companies trying to make the best quality chocolate possible, and Zander decided that approach had to be brought to Israel.

How does one start making chocolate from scratch? The first problem was machinery. DeVries was quite open about what he was doing, but not all others were forthcoming.

The first steps were to go back to basics. "The chocolate business has been hijacked by these big companies," explains Zander. The industry giants are based on mass production with appropriate equipment, so

Zander set out to find very old machinery to accommodate small quantities. He searched antique stores, and he began to improvise. In 2008 Zander bought his first piece of equipment, a grinding machine capable of dealing with forty pounds of cocoa beans at a time. The next item was to transform a Maytag dryer into a bean roaster.

At the beginning of 2010 "Holy Cacao" became a formal business. Zander and his new partner, Zev Stender formerly of Woodmere, moved into a formal facility in the industrial section of Pnei Hever, a little-known settlement in the Hebron Hills. The organizational stage was over. It was time for commercial production. Rabbinical supervision (O-U *pareve* and made kosher for Passover throughout the year) was added. The beans are checked for infestation, but mold is more common.

Eight types of chocolate became the company's standards: Gianduja (containing pistachio), Mexican (with almonds, cinnamon and chili), Coffee (with Ethiopian coffee roasted in-house), Dominican bar (from cacao grown in the Dominican Republic), and Peruvian bars of 72 percent, 91 percent, and 100 percent cacao (from a small cacao farm bought by Holy Cacao in late 2010). Yes, there really is a difference in taste between cacao grown in the Caribbean and in the Andes!

Zander's company is obviously new, and there are experiments with new products. Their chocolate covered dates are delicious (made under private label), and occasionally other products are made on a trial basis.

Tempted by a quality chocolate made personally, as the saying goes, "From bean to bar?" Jo Zander accepts pre-arranged tours of his factory as the production schedule and his *daf yomi* learning permit, with sales on the premises. The Holy Cacao bars are also available in selected Israeli health stores (they are organic).

Jo Zander found a unique way to observe mitzvot and keep kosher as he entered the food business.

To the East of Jerusalem

Maaleh Adumim

This is a city 7 kilometers east of Jerusalem that started in 1975 with twenty-three families and now numbers over thirty-seven thousand residents. The name is taken from verses in the Book of Joshua, which describe the border between Judah and Benjamin as containing red rocks.

A noted archeological site developed in the 1980s is the Christian Martyrius Monastery, named after Martyrius of Cappadocia (Turkey), who served as the Greek Orthodox Patriarch of Jerusalem (478–486 CE). The monastery has no Jewish significance whatsoever. It was damaged during the Persian invasion in 614 CE and was deserted after the Arab conquest in the mid-seventh century. The building decayed during centuries of disuse.

Moshe Castel Museum of Art
(See color plate 10, p 100)

Many religious people are almost ambivalent to art and often view it in somewhat degrading terms. Perhaps this is due to common non-Jewish motifs in classic paintings or an offensive immodesty that is sometimes depicted. Yet, there is a strong Jewish tradition in art dating back to Bezalel and Biblical times. Paintings and drawings, when used properly, can convey an effective religious message. That is what Moshe Castel (1909–1991) has done.

Castel (taken from "Castella," or "Spain") was a fifteenth generation resident of Eretz Yisrael. His family arrived in Gaza following the Spanish Inquisition, then as the centuries passed they moved to Hebron. During the 1929 riots his uncle was murdered, and the family fled to Jerusalem and Tsfat.

Childhood years made a strong impression on Castel. Several times he drew pictures of his distinguished father, a scribe, cantor, teacher, poet in Ladino and artisan in his own right, and after whom a synagogue is named in Machane Yehudah. Curiously, the father also made the covering on the tombstone of Aharon HaCohen in Jordan's Petra Enclave. Even at an early age his artistic talents were recognized, and after excelling in the Bezalel School of Art, at age sixteen he was sent to Paris to develop his skills. At one point the renowned Jewish leader, Ze'ev Jabotinsky (1880-1940), came to see the artwork of this artist from Eretz Yisrael.

It is hard to describe the many works of Moshe Castel. One that he produced is a very moving oil painting depicting the *Aron Kodesh* in the Ari Synagogue in Tsfat, with light emanating from the *Sifrei Torah*. The message is clear that the Torah enlightens our existence.

Castel's perspective was most definitely religious, with emphasis on Jerusalem and with a touch of mysticism. Another of his paintings ("Ancient Scrolls," 1940, oil on canvas) on display in the museum shows the continuity of Torah from the *Akeida* (Binding of Isaac) in the lower part of the picture through the much later story of Purim shown above. The painting also expresses the post–WWII sentiment of progressing from imminent slaughter to total triumph.

There is one interesting religious statement to be inferred from the *Akeida*. In the shadows near Yitzchak there is the very vague figure of a woman. This is Castel's way of suggesting that although Sarah was not physically present, her psychological support never wavered. A mother always pays attention to her child.

Some of Castel's pictures are not exactly serious. Not only did Mordechai reject the grandeur of Haman and refuse to bow down to him. One work shows Esther displaying a comically mocking disrespect for the arch-villain.

There are also paintings that are not realistic. "Olive Gathering" (1940) shows an idealistic view of the harvest with no one toiling under the summer heat. But isn't that realism? Is it not the idealized childhood memories of a boy growing up in Palestine?

Another painting illustrates a religious figure speaking or perhaps singing with letters of the ancient Hebrew script rising to the heavens and descending. This is a trigger for thought. Our heritage of ancient writing should not be forgotten. We maintain a communication of praise with the Al-mighty. Our very presence in this world is a result of speech, since Creation was the result of words, as G-d said there will be, and there was.

The cornerstone for this museum was laid in 1992, but work proceeded slowly according to the architectural plans of David Reznik (also Resnick; 1924-2012). Only in March 2010 was worked completed. In the year following the opening more than seven thousand visitors enjoyed the fine collection of Castel's monumental works. Although art is the main theme of the museum, Reznik's architecture with magnificent views of the Judean Hills and Jerusalem on the horizon are not to be neglected.

Not all of Castel's art is on display in the museum. As the Nazis advanced toward Paris, Castel fled, leaving his art behind. After the war

Castel found nothing. All had been destroyed or stolen. Today Castel's art can also be seen in the Knesset, the Weizmann Institute, Binyanei HaUmah (International Convention Centre), the Technion and other prestigious places.

The museum is definitely recommended. It is a fine example of yet another method of religious expression. It is not a museum to race through. Sit, look, think, and let the artwork speak.

Open Sunday-Thursday 1000–1700 except Tuesday until 1900. Friday and holiday eves 1000–1400. Closed Shabbat and holidays. Admission: Adults NIS36, Seniors and Disabled NIS18, Families NIS100. Telephone: 02-535-7000. Fax: 02-535-6600. Wheelchair accessible.

Mishor Adumim

This is the industrial zone of Maale Adumim. It is an excellent place to find hard-to-get items direct from manufacturers. There are also two large supermarkets, the main branch of a major commercial cake bakery, food production companies, and several wineries. The Industrial Park Development Corporation, immediately to the left past security inspection when entering from the Maaleh Adumim–Jericho Road, maintains computerized lists of all business according to type.

Maya Foods

Morris Waysman, Managing Director of Maya Foods, is one of three childhood friends who founded Maya in 1984. He has been with the company since they started in Jerusalem's Givat Shaul neighborhood with legumes and spices, then expanded to their current complex in Mishor Adumim where some 800 or so items are packaged and/or produced.

All of the company's products are certified by the Eida Chareidit, even though for marketing reasons or for private label packaging, another supervision sometimes appears. This is particularly true for Passover when, based on historical reasons, the Eida declines to give certification, although they do certify those products for non-Passover *chametz* purposes.

Beans are just one of the many Maya products. Is Eida kashrut supervision just a marketing gimmick? Clearly it is not! As the Maya CEO explains, supervision starts in the field with examination not only for size and type, but also for cleaning and infestation. Using lima beans as an example, rabbis are sent to Italy and Uruguay when beans are purchased from those countries.

As the beans arrive in Mishor Adumim, the kashrut supervisor certifies that what has arrived is what was sent. The food laboratory also inspects technical specifications, such as the percentage of ash, size, color, weight, shape, and deformities. In a joint operation the *mashgiach* places a sample of the beans in water, and that is kept in the laboratory for twelve hours as part of the process of checking for infestation. Imported beans that are rejected are covered by insurance, sold to non-Jewish markets, or destroyed—depending upon the exact nature of the problem.

Inspection at the entrance to the Maya plant is just the beginning of a long process. Sieves again check size and catch leaves and other debris. Even a metal detector is used back up the sieves and to ascertain that a piece of machinery did not fall into the beans. When the beans leave the factory they are clean of dirt and bugs, with the possible exception of some microscopic eggs which scientific methods have been unable to clean until now.

Maya has has developed and received health approval for an innovative stems to kill microscopic eggs. This is a new product line in vacuum packaging, Maya Select, has recently been introduced on the market. For one month the products are exposed to biological treatment prior to packaging; there is then a one year guarantee that eggs will not develop. According to the CEO, the treatment and the vacuum packaging do not affect taste. This is only one example of how Maya tries to reach the highest kashrut standards.

Does the general consumer know what he is buying? Purchasing beans is not a simple matter even when setting kashrut aside. White beans, for example, come in different sizes, weights, and shades of white. They are typically grown in such different places as Argentina, Canada, and China. Yes, there is a difference in taste. Argentine beans command a higher price.

When the package of beans arrives home, what happens next? The incubation period for many insects is three weeks. In other words, three weeks after the package leaves Maya there is a possibility of infestation. The best storage to prevent infestation is in the refrigerator. The pantry, without the heat and humidity of the kitchen, is better than the cooking area. (Optimum temperature for infestation is about 30°C.) Every package of Maya beans is labeled that the contents should be checked before use. This is an explicit requirement of the Eida supervision, and it is advice based upon the Maya company experience. It is not a matter of checking beans sold in Israel but not those sold in the United States or the United Kingdom. Beans must always be checked for bugs! There are lima beans grown in Israel under strict health rules. They, too, must be checked for bugs even after examination in the packaging plant.

Rice is another example of a Maya product. Choosing rice is also not as simple as it might seem. In very simplistic terms, Basmati rice that is grown in India and Pakistan has a tender taste that is best when preparing recipes from the Sub-Continent. Italian Risotto rice tends to absorb flavor; it is the best to use when making sushi. (There is an alternative method of steaming long grain rice to make it sticky.) Most European dishes are to be preferred with long grain rice. But, with which long grain rice?

Rice in England usually comes from Thailand, the United States, Uruguay, and even Spain. Israel imports most of its rice from Thailand and Vietnam. Jasmine rice is of better quality than "Persian" rice, a marketing name that has nothing to do with Iran. For the record, the United States is the biggest producer of rice. Australia also produces large quantities.

In all rice production the outer, non-edible casing is removed in the country of origin. That shell is not totally discarded. In most cases it is salvaged for use as a fuel. Usually in the country of packaging an inner shell is removed; when it remains, that rice is called whole grain. The shell that is removed at this stage is often sold for animal feed. Whole grain rice (with the inner shell) is healthier, but it is more susceptible to infestation, since there is less cleaning.

After the inner shell is removed, "white rice" is polished either once or twice depending on the quality desired. Other factors in quality are starch content, whiteness, length, and weight. If you buy generically packaged "rice," you are certainly buying rice, but it is with less quality control.

Precautions must be taken to insure that the rice—all kinds of rice—is not infested with bugs. "Carolina," a large American company, fumigates its rice, a process that requires very exacting health standards. Maya looks at samples by soaking them for twelve hours in water, then still says that consumers should check for bugs hatched after leaving the factory. The recommended methods are soaking, examination on a light table, or looking at the rice on a tray.

Some companies market "Quick Rice" that takes less time to cook. This can be a quality product, but the consumer has to realize that the reason for "quick" is that the rice has already been partially cooked (which should be under appropriate supervision according to many rabbis.) Another issue with an obvious kashrut implications is that rice with added spices and/or flavorings needs careful supervision.

Industry sources recommend that brown rice can ideally be stored in cool (but not refrigerated) conditions for up to eighteen months. White rice can be stored for two years. Vacuum packed rice, however, can be stored for much longer until it is opened. It should be remembered that the longer the storage, the greater the possibility of infestation. Conversely, the shorter the storage, the more vitamin yield the product will have.

Are you willing to buy just any package of beans or rice? Perhaps beans or rice with supervision of a lower standard, since they are raw? That is certainly not the advice of Morris Waysman (nor of the Eida Chareidit).

At this time there are no tours available of the Maya plant, however the company's products are widely available in stores throughout Israel.

Taaman Foods

Every company tries to find its own unique niche in the market, and Taaman, a enterprise owned by religious Jews and headquartered in Mishor Adumim, is no different. As company director Shalom Haim explains, Taaman is based upon reliable supply of quality *mehadrin* products at reasonable prices. Although that might sound simple, running the business is much more complicated.

Initial experience began in 1978, when operations started in space near the old Jerusalem railroad station. The method of sales was straightforward—buy and sell. There were no imports and no market analyses. The stress was on industrial oils. Find a buyer, find a supplier, and sell. Then in 1999, with experience accrued and lessons learnt, Taaman moved to Mishor Adumim and started virtually anew.

Soon Taaman grew to be an international company dealing in imports and exports. In the United Kingdom, for example, Taaman is distributed by Drumstick. The rationale of international scope is simple. All Taaman products are *mehadrin*, and all foodstuffs with the flagstaff "Taaman" label carry Eida supervision regardless of where they are sold. Sending *mashgichim* from Israel (Eida policy) costs money. Haim provides an example. Kashrut requirements to produce tuna to fill one container will add 20 percent to the price of each can; filling twenty containers will add only one percent to the cost. Hence, the key to competitive pricing is in quantity. The key to quantity is in expanding the market and selling in as many places (countries) as possible.

For the record, Taaman tuna is of the "skipjack" species (*katsuwonus pelamis)*, prevalent also on Israeli supermarket shelves. "Albacore" (*thunnus alalunga*) is popular in the United States, but it is much more expensive. Another factor in the price of tuna is the proportion of solid tuna and tuna flakes in each can. In pondering which tuna to buy, another consideration is the type of oil. One should be aware that some kosher supervision services inspect each and every fish for scales and fins, whereas others pay a bounty to non-Jewish workers for finding non-kosher fish in the nets.

Some Taaman products never reach Israeli shores. The Taaman grape juice sold in England is made in Spain (under Eida supervision). Due to European Union customs rules, that grape juice is less expensive than Israeli imports in England. (Spanish grapes are of renowned quality, and several companies import them for wine and juice bottled in Israel.)

No, Taaman does not have its own production lines. It works on contracts with various companies which produce their three hundred to four hundred products. Some products come from abroad, such as pasta (Turkey), olive oil (Spain), and cornflakes (Argentina), for which Israeli production is too small to be competitive, though packaging is often carried out at Taaman Mishor Adumim. As one would expect, there still is no gefilte fish "Made in China." Gefilte fish is one of the many Taaman Israeli products.

A basic principle in Taaman's operation is that they are able to switch contractors when a better deal becomes available. They are not encumbered by owning production lines that become out-of-date or obsolete.

Unique Passover foods such as cookies, all manufactured exclusively in Israel, provide special problems. But, what happens to leftovers, usually between 10 and 15 percent of stock, after the holiday? Cookies that sell for NIS30 or NIS40 per kilo before Passover cannot be sold for even NIS2 afterwards. As Shalom Haim explains, nothing is trashed. Cookies are donated to various charities.

In some cases products have a Passover "stigma" and cannot be sold to consumers. Chocolate spread, for example, is made with a different oil (usually hazelnut)—tasty, but not wanted after the holiday. Taaman sells off their unwanted remains to institutions at highly reduced prices. Ironically, Nutella® is a popular international chocolate spread (not *mehadrin*) based upon the same hazelnut oil.

In 2011 (5771) it was extremely difficult if not impossible in Israel to find *mehadrin* walnut oil for Passover. Why? The previous year's production was sold at a higher price than the market could bear due to costs of importing from the United States. Thus, Taaman and apparently other companies as well decided not to run the risk of another loss; they did not import walnut oil. For the same reason there was no walnut oil mayonnaise to be found. Although quite tasty, in 2010 the price was three times that of hazelnut and palm oil mayonnaise, resulting in 30 percent returns.

In Israel you might see supermarket labels with fine print that the item was produced by Taaman. The technique is for marketing purposes only. Canola oil, for example, is exactly the same. Only the label is different.

There are no tours of the Taaman factory at this time, nor is there an on-site company store for direct sales to the public.

Zion (Shorr) and HaCormim Wineries – See Kosher Wine Guide

Pundak Hashomroni Hatov Mosaics Museum

This site, transferred in late 2010 to the Parks Authority, is a problematic tourist attraction for religious Jews. Seeing the outside excavation and Exhibit Halls I, II, and III poses no religious objection. The general site, however, is advertised with a Christian orientation based upon a non-Jewish religious tradition and church themes in the remaining exhibit halls. The decision regarding visiting is best left to be personal.

In recent years this museum has been transformed into a collection point for many of the mosaic floors unearthed in Israel. The exhibits begin with mosaics from the Samaritans, who separated normative Judaism in the period of the First Temple, if not before. An example is the synagogue mosaic found in Khirbet Samara, a city that once existed just south of the Nablus-Tulkarem Road near today's Einav. The mosaic, with flora and the seven species, was recovered from what had been a synagogue evidently built in the fourth century CE over the ruins of a Roman building. The building was possibly destroyed after the Third Samaritan Revolt in the fifth century CE.

It is amazing how the Samaritan community, once numbering tens of thousands and a presence as far away as the Greek island of Delos, has dwindled to a mere several hundred. Another item on display is a Samaritan mosaic (evidently fourth to fifth century CE) recovered in 1949 from Sha'alvim near the Latrun Interchange, and far from traditional Samaria.

Not all is Samaritan. The museum exhibit contains a mosaic in Aramaic from a Jewish synagogue in Na'aran (fifth or sixth century CE) and another from Estamoa (fourth or fifth century CE). Perhaps the most famous mosaic on display is from the sixth or seventh century CE in a Gaza synagogue; the mosaic displays King David.

Hours: Open daily 0800–1600. Adults NIS20, Children (5–18) NIS10. Wheelchair accessible with difficulty due to a dirt and gravel parking lot. Bathrooms are not suitable for wheelchairs. For additional information: Telephone: 02-541-7555

To the West of Jerusalem

Nebi Samuel

Nebi Samuel, the Arabic name by which the grave of Samuel the Prophet is popularly known, lies less than a kilometer into the West Bank, and across the Green Line from the Jerusalem neighborhood of Ramot. It is within *techum Shabbat* (the distance from the edge of town that one is permitted to walk), but for many reasons it is hard to find a *minyan* there on Shabbat. During the week, however, this is a common site for Jewish prayer (on the lower storey, below the main floor of the mosque).

The area has not only religious, but also strategic importance. In 1192, Richard the Lion-Hearted (Richard I; 1157-1199) used this hill as a staging point in preparation for his attack on Jerusalem during the Third Crusade. His plan, though, was abandoned, when reinforcements failed to arrive. It appears that a church stood on the site at about that time. Several centuries later there was a synagogue, which has been restored on the lower level. Now the mosque and minaret built in 1730 over the prophet's grave are blatant features in the skyline overlooking Jerusalem, since they command the highest natural point in the area.

More recently, Nebi Samuel was the site of intense fighting in 1917, as the British conquered an Ottoman military base and moved on to capture Jerusalem. Then, the British established their own base on the spot during the Mandate. Not to be outflanked, today the IDF also has a presence on the same hill.

There were Jewish efforts to settle the hill in the 1890s, but security problems caused the project to be abandoned. A 1930s project also failed. Part of the mosque and the minaret tower were destroyed in British–Ottoman fighting in 1917; repairs to the structures were subsequently made.

Beit Iksa is the neighboring Arab village, whose name is a testimony to history. *Iksa* is the Roman numeral, "X," and the name immortalizes what was once the camping ground of the Roman Tenth Legion. Rome was an occupying power, and their forces were spread throughout Jerusalem. (An alternative explanation is that Beit Iksa is named after a local thief, who built a house here.)

Another Tenth Legion installation has been uncovered in the lower level of the Binyanei HaUmah (Israel Convention Center) expansion opposite the Central Bus Station. The Tenth Legion had numerous construction and public works functions. For example, a series of kilns to produce earthenware has been found.

One intriguing site near the mosque is Kolel Shmuel HaNavi, an innovative dream of HaRav Moshe Amoyal, an Israeli-born rabbi of Moroccan descent. Verbal tradition recalls a promise by Samuel the Prophet that the prayers of all who pray in his name will be answered. That attracted not only those wanting to pray, but also HaRav Amoyal, who started a *kolel* in 1989. Slowly but surely the *kolel* began to attract students; then came innovation.

The commandment is to learn Torah *yomam va'laylah*—not only during the day, but also at night. So, HaRav Amoyal added Kolel Chatsos, a group of dedicated students who grouped near the grave of Shmuel HaNavi to learn from midnight, until 0800. Another group started to learn *b-ashmoret ha-boqer* (the last third of the night), then prayed at sunrise, *k'vatikin*. The lower floor of the mosque took on a living Jewish flavor, and to the lasting credit of HaRav Amoyal, no real problems were ever encountered with Moslem neighbors.

Now the once-thriving *kolel* of more than thirty-five men coming to learn has dwindled down to a small handful learning *issur va-heter*, and financial problems are threatening its closure. The *kolel* has been forced from the main building into a caravan supplied by the IDF and placed outside a perimeter fence. The charity boxes that were the cornerstone of financial viability were taken down from the walls near the grave of the Prophet. Also, tourists rarely come to the area to drop a small donation into the one box that remains just outside the *kolel*.

The Israel Antiquities Authority has transformed the land surrounding the mosque into a large maze of archeological excavations. Even entrance into the mosque and the grave are via a pedestrian bridge that hovers over a dig. The area has been designated a national park. The minaret with its commanding outlook is now closed to the public, as are many of the excavations.

It is not only the tourists who no longer come. There no longer are vans bringing Jerusalemites to pray at sunrise, *k'vatikin*. The building is no longer open throughout the night. Hours are now restricted, as befitting any "historical museum." But, for HaRav Moshe Amoyal and for those Jewish faithful who still come to offer their prayers, the virtue of praying and learning in the name of Shmuel HaNavi will never be forgotten.

Note: Visiting hours to Kolel Shmuel HaNavi can be ascertained from the *kolel* at telephone number 02-586-2375. The *kever* is not within the *eruv* for carrying on Shabbat.

El-Jib

Just to the west is the Arab village of El-Jib, the site of Biblical Giv'on. The ancient *tel* has not been fully excavated. At the summit a water source with seventy-nine steps leading to it was found, but exact dating is uncertain. In nearby excavations that have been carried out in seasons during 1956–1966, James B. Pritchard (1909–1997) unearthed more than sixty wine cellars from the seventh and eighth centuries BCE and two water systems including shaft and tunnel.

There are numerous burial caves in the area, and it appears that at least part of today's village is built on ancient burial grounds.

The site is not well developed for tourism. A visit to El-Jib is also not recommended for security reasons.

Beit Horon

The name of this place is evidently derived from Horon, the appellation of a supposed god worshiped by the Canaanites. References to Beit Horon can be found in Joshua 10:10-11 and elsewhere. Adjacent are the Arab villages of Upper Beit Oor and Lower Beit Oor. This recalls Chronicles I 7:24 and Chronicles II 8:5, which cite Upper and Lower Beit Horon.

This modern settlement initiated in 1977 along Route 443 was another village of strategic importance on an ancient Roman road. In 166 BCE a battle was fought here between the soldiers of Judah Maccabee and the Seleucid Empire. The Jewish forces were triumphant in good measure due to their exacting knowledge of the topography. After the Bar Kochba rebellion the road was improved significantly to allow troops to move quickly and freely. Even today there are numerous historical remains along the ancient highway. The exact identification of some of the remains is in doubt; others are very partial and of lesser interest to the average tourist.

Today Beit Horon is an important facility for the Israel Police as well as home to more than six hundred residents, both religious and secular.

Kfar Hashmonaim

From modest beginnings in 1978 Zohar Bar'am has slowly transformed twenty-three dunhams of barren land into a fascinating reconstruction of life in the Neolithic, Sinai Wandering, Hasmonean, and Roman periods. The secret to this "walk through history" is Bar'am's hands-on approach, encouraging children to understand the past through "doing."

A tour with Zohar Bar'am is an extraordinary experience with exposure to a rich variety of information. A bit of historic trivia, for example—ancient settlers often cultivated lemons and pomegranates, since these plants yield fruits relatively quickly.

There are too many exhibits to list. Just one—a sundial based upon the shadow cast by a nail accurately indicates the hour of the day.

At different stages children are encouraged to chip away stone by using another stone to illustrate ancient "cutting." They are given the opportunity to make a mosaic design in imitation of ancient procedures. They even can strike a rock and see water come forth. (For adults there is a much more sophisticated message, as Bar'am explains how plants can grow in rocks and why they are often used for medicinal purposes.) One exhibit illustrates the development of the Hebrew script. There is a house, typical of the Second Temple period, and also a synagogue.

How are seals to "sign" a message made? There is a hands-on demonstration. The resulting seal is a souvenir to take home.

To reach Kfar Hashmonaim travel on Route 443. Turn at the Shilat Junction, then turn left at the shopping center. Signs lead to the site. Admission is NIS30 for adults, NIS35 for children. Groups NIS700. Visits by prior arrangement. Sabbath visits are permitted, however finances must be arranged in advance although actual payment can be later; there are also no arts and crafts activities on Shabbat. Tours are given by Zohar Bar'am in Hebrew and/or English and generally last slightly less than three hours for children.

One word of advice. Although this site is excellent for children, adults will enjoy it as well!

Kfar Ruth

This small *moshav* noted on the sixth century Madaba map was re-established in 1977. To the east of the *moshav* there are remains of a Roman guard station with a view to the ancient road to Jerusalem. There is also an ancient wine press that has been discovered.

Ruth Winery – See Kosher Wine Guide

Kharruba

The remains of a Roman era fortress that guarded the road to Jerusalem can be seen here, eight kilometers east of Ramla. Tradition has been passed down that the Bar Kochba Revolt started in Kharruba.

Mevo Modi'in

Today's Mevo Modi'in is a unique *moshav* just off Route 443. The highway is relatively new, dating only to the 1980s, but in ancient times what is now Mevo Modi'in (also spelt Modi'im) was on the Roman Road to Jerusalem. Mevo Modi'in was an important stronghold overlooking this road. (see Beit Horon).

The modern religious *moshav* was founded in 1976 by the rabbi/ singer Shlomo Carlebach (1925–1994), who lived there during his lifetime between traveling world-wide to do *kiruv* work. Services in the synagogue are basically Carlebach-style. Although Carlebach studied in great yeshivas and was granted rabbinic ordination by the late Rabbi Yitzchak Hutner (1906–1980), he is best known for his more than two dozen musical albums and prayer tunes which are popular worldwide.

There are very talented artists in the small *moshav*, including a silversmith, painters and potters. Pizza is available from 1600 to 2200 (in the *moshav* at the far end of the roundabout), and falafel is sold in a trailer (at the entrance to the *moshav*) from 1000 to 1700. Both places are under the *mehadrin* supervision of Rabbi Hoffman, the rabbi of Mevo Modi'in. Healthy farm meals are available by pre-order at the Chai Farm (see immediately below).

The local synagogue is decorated with impressive hand paintings by Yitzchak Ben Yehuda, a world-renowned painter and local resident. He has a fascinating Egyptian background, discovering only in his mid-twenties that he was born to a Jewish mother.

Behind the synagogue and up the stairs there are ancient ruins containing wine and olive presses from the Hasmonean, Roman, and Byzantine periods based on construction styles and coins recovered at the scene.

Chai Hands-on Goat Farm

The farm started in 2009 and is run under the Maccabi Institute Charity. It maintains a herd of thirty-five goats (and growing) from which organic cheese products are produced. The cheeses are not sold on the general market, but in season they are available "for tasting" by visitors.

Children learn to milk goats and make cheese. There are also spinning and weaving, clay work, batik nature picture, wheat grinding and olive pressing, hiking and guided tours in Hebrew or English. The tour is good for all ages. There is no question that visiting this farm with children is a "sure winner."

To arrange a visit, call 054-428-3646. Prices range from NIS40–NIS60 (discounts available for educational groups and for the handicapped) preferably with groups of at least six. Sometimes smaller groups are combined. Closed on the Sabbath, holidays, and Chol Hamoed

Modi'in

The exact location of ancient Modi'in, famous from the history of the MaccabeeMacabees, is a matter of conjecture. One possibility is Um el Umdan, on the Modi'in-Latrun road. There archeologists discovered an ancient synagogue and what is thought to be a Hasmonean village, including houses, a *mikva*, a once-plush villa and a market. Apparently there was also a bath for Roman soldiers. Some archeologists believe that the synagogue is the oldest ever discovered, based in part on items from the Persian, Hasmonean and Roman periods.

Another plausible possibility for ancient Modi'in is Tetora Hill on the northeast edge of Modi'in, where there are the remains of a Crusader watchtower built atop of ruins dating from the Hasmonean period. Within the city limits there are also numerous caves generally not suitable for tourism, some with (unverified) historical traditions.

Construction of modern Modi'in started in 1993, and now there are more than 70,000 residents. It is a city planned by Moshe Safdie (1938–). Although there are religious Jews in Modi'in, they do not set the tone of the city.

Since 2008 Modi'in has been served by a train operating to Ben Gurion Airport, Tel Aviv, and other coastal points. Service to Jerusalem is expected in 2016. The railroad station is entirely underground (the only such station in Israel), but do not try to drive there. The station does not have a parking lot. Travelers can either walk or take a bus to the station.

Industrial Zone

In the Shoham Forest near the Modi'in Industrial Zone are the Nabalat ruins with carvings, olive presses, and ancient mosaics.

Maccabee Graves

A sign on the northern side of Route 443 indicates the Graves of the Maccabees. The authenticity of the site is in serious doubt, and there are several suggestions of other locations. The tradition of Maccabee burial in the area of Modi'in is recorded on the sixth century Madaba map; an exact location, however, cannot be ascertained from the map.

Modi'in Illit (Kiryat Sefer)

Kiryat Sefer, the popular name for the more legalistic "Modi'in Illit," is an orthodox city located midway between Jerusalem and Tel Aviv. It is some twenty-five kilometers east of Tel Aviv on a hill accessible to the ancient road from Caesarea via Beit Horon to Jerusalem. It was settled at least as early as the Book of Judges. During excavations to build the modern city remnants of a Jewish village were found on today's Rechov Mesilat Yosef. Analysis of the remains shows that several houses were arranged around a broad square, at the center of which stood a synagogue, though it is hard for the non-professional to envision the ancient settlement (closed to the public by a fence).

The buildings were well-constructed and separated by narrow alleys; their walls made of large, trimmed stones, and the entrances of well-dressed ashlars. Each house consisted of several rooms around an inner courtyard. In them were various installations, such as pits for storing water, cut into the rock to considerable depth, olive presses with stone basins for crushing and heavy stone weights for pressing. The *mikva'ot* in the houses were cut into the rock and plastered, with stairs leading to the bottom, suggesting observance of ritual purity. The synagogue was a modest structure, implying not a very affluent population. Curiously, the synagogue was apparently not built with prayer in the direction of Jerusalem.

Kiryat Sefer was abandoned in the course of the First Jewish Revolt against Rome (66–70 CE). It was soon resettled, but was laid to ruin by the Romans during the Bar-Kochba Rebellion (132–135 CE).

The modern city was first populated in 1994, and the local council of Modi'in Illit was given city status on March 7, 2008.

Zagłębie Memorial

Along Route 443 on the southern side between Modi'in and Ben Shemen (turn off at Mevo Modi'in) is a Jewish National Fund (JNF) forest and memorial to the Jews of Zagłębie. Before World War II more than one hundred thousand Jews lived in the Zagłębie region in southern Poland, but on August 12, 1942 the Nazis started a round-up for selection. Disgracefully, Moshe Merlin, chairman of the Judenrat, assisted the Nazis in hope of saving his own life; he was paid in kind and eventually deported to Auschwitz, never to return. Twelve thousand five hundred Jews were transported to Auschwitz to be murdered immediately; those determined to be fit for work were assigned to slave labor camps, where most died. The forest and memorial plaque are dedicated to the memory of all of those who perished.

Jerusalem Corridor

An Overview of History

The land stretching from Jerusalem to the approaches to Latrun has become to be known as the Jerusalem Corridor, what upon independence in 1948 was literally a narrow lifeline to Israel's capital. As such it saw many fierce and bloody battles with Arab forces. After the War of Independence Jews were settled in the corridor for defensive purposes. The idea was not to build forts and fortresses, but rather to establish a permanent and sustainable civilian Jewish presence.

Hiking, Biking, and Mountain Paths

Hiking Paths

The most famous hiking route in Israel is the Israel Path, initiated in 1994 and covering 840 kilometers from Beit Ussishkin near Kibbutz Dan in the north to the Red Sea in the south. For those who are adventurous, the entire trek usually takes about six to eight weeks. It is a challenge. Estimates are that only about one in four hikers actually finishes the trek.

For the more modest hiker, a segment of the path passes through the area covered by this book, taking in Sha'alvim, Latrun and the Sataf, with pleasant walks though JNF forests. The path is well marked. Short segments can make for a pleasant day's outing.

There are several other marked hiking paths in the Judean Hills. These paths have three parallel stripes, usually painted on rocks or trees. A bent marking means to walk in the direction of the bend. Even though there are markings, taking along a map is always a good idea.

Another hiking opportunity is the 42 km. Jerusalem Path that was initiated in 2006 and stretches from the Sataf into Jerusalem, then ends near Hadassah Hospital in Ein Karem.

These paths do not have large numbers of hikers, except in certain popular sections. It is recommended to take an ample supply of food and drink, comfortable shoes, a hat with a brim, and a mobile phone in case of emergency.

Biking Paths

There are numerous biking paths ("BF" – Biking Friendly) in the Judean Hills and Beit Shemesh area. A map in Hebrew and English (not all is translated) is available by calling 08-850-2240. The map also lists sites of interest and the difficulty of each path (easy, intermediate, difficult).

Mountain Paths

Maslul BaHar is a small company headquartered in Moshav Givat Yearim. The company offers "off the beaten track" tours in the Judean Hills. Arrangements can be made by calling 054-767-7634.

JNF Forests

There are numerous JNF forests in the Judean Hills. Many have various picnic areas and scenic vantage points. Maps and brochures can be obtained at the Information Centers in Yad Kennedy (Amminadav Forest) and the Sataf, or by calling 02-563-5638.

Driving Routes

There is a wine route, going from winery to winery. The scenery is breathtaking, however the path as a tour of wineries is not recommended, since a large number of the wineries are small companies and do not have kashrut certification.

Memorials to the Fallen

Bus 405

On July 6, 1989 an Islamic Jihad member grabbed the steering wheel of a bus from Tel-Aviv to Jerusalem, causing the bus to fall into the nearby ravine. Fourteen people were pronounced dead at the scene, and another two died in hospital. Thirty others were wounded.

The incident took place on the highway opposite the Telshe Stone yeshiva, and students rushed out to help. That spontaneous response was the impetus for HaRav Elazar Gelbstein to start *Chesed Shel Emet,* which later evolved into ZAKA, first a police Civil Guard unit, then a non-profit independent organization.

Today just south of the Tel Aviv-Jerusalem Highway opposite Telshe Stone there is a monument to memorialize the victims. Parking is very difficult, thus limiting access.

The perpetrator, Abed al-Hadi Ghanayem, was sentenced to sixteen life sentences for murder and hijacking. (He was released as part of the 2011 exchange for Gilad Schalit.)

Convoys to Jerusalem

There are several burnt-out but repainted remains of armored vehicles along the Jerusalem–Tel Aviv Highway, kept to memorialize the battle for access to Jerusalem and the four hundred fighters who were killed. The vehicles are along the highway between Shaar Ha-gai and Shoeva junctions. The effort to supply Jerusalem was dangerous but critical to the Jewish presence in the city. Most drivers were volunteers, who risked their lives in both directions.

The convoys were extremely vulnerable. The Arab tactic was very simple. Piles of stones were placed across the road, forcing the drivers to halt. Then snipers hidden between the rocks in the hills near the road would open fire on the riders and vehicles.

Most of the trucks belonged to various kibbutz cooperative transport companies. Supplies were covered with canvas and tied in the back of the trucks. Although the trucks were plated with metal, many of the people in the convoys, drivers and passengers alike, lost their lives.

During the War of Independence, 230 convoys traveled to Jerusalem, but only eight convoys were forced to turn back. These convoys comprised more than 3,100 trucks.

Forest of the Martyrs

In the Eshtaol Forest near Beit Meir there is a memorial to the six million Jews who were murdered during the Holocaust. The memorial is highlighted by a bronze sculpture, Scroll of Fire, made by Nathan Rappaport (1911–1987). Others of his Holocaust-related sculptures are on display in the United States, Poland, and various places in Israel.

Abu Ghosh

To the west of the Qastel along the main road is Abu Ghosh, an Arab village of slightly less than six thousand inhabitants. Abu Ghosh is thought by many to be the biblical site of Kiryat Ye'arim, one of the four cities of Giv'on. Archeological evidence suggests that the area was inhabited even before then. A Greek inscription unearthed in the ruins of a Roman fort shows that part of the Tenth Legion of the Roman army was stationed in Abu Ghosh. During the Crusader period Christian forces built a church there.

The name, Abu Ghosh, is based upon a clan who settled in the area in the sixteenth century. In 1948 the village remained neutral, if not siding with Israel. Primarily for that reason the basically Cherkess residents did not become refugees. The current local council was organized in 1993.

Several times it was a resident of Abu Ghosh who bought the *chametz* of the State of Israel for the Passover period.

Beit Meir

In Beit Meir there is a "Shabbat Farm," an educational effort to demonstrate the thirty-nine *melachot* of Shabbat primarily as they relate to agriculture.

A two-hour presentation in English or Hebrew, designed for children, is available by calling 02-533-2455 or 050-633-3747. Fee is NIS35 per person. Not wheelchair accessible.

HaMasrek Winery – See Winery Guide

Beit Zait

This *moshav* just behind Motza off the Jerusalem-Tel Aviv Highway was founded in 1949 in an effort to populate and defend the area adjacent to the road. In the *moshav* there are foot imprints in stone judged by some to be from a dinosaur (*elaphrosaurs bambergi janensch* species).

Givat Yeshaiahu

This is a small *moshav* established in 1958 by immigrants from Hungary and located about ten kilometers south of Beit Shemesh.

Of particular interest is an archeology park nearby. There the JNF and the Israel Antiquities Authority jointly sponsor day-long digs that teach methodology. The program is only by prior arrangement by calling 02-992-1136 or 052-428-4405.

Har Tay(y)asim

Further westward from the back entrance to the Sataf and just off Route 395 is Har Tay(y)asim with a monument constructed in the late 1990s in memory of the fallen soldiers of the IDF Air Force. All of those who perished during their service are listed by name. A push-button audio recording with explanation in Hebrew and English is available. There is also an excellent view of the Judean Hills.

A 6.9 kilometer circular hiking path of moderate difficulty is nearby.

Mevasseret Tzion

In 1951 immigrants from Kurdistan, Iran, and North Africa were settled to the south of the Jerusalem–Tel Aviv Highway at the foot of the Qastel (see below). Five years later immigrants from North Africa were settled to the north of the highway. In 1963 the two neighborhoods were joined together as Mevasseret Tzion, today an affluent suburb of Jerusalem.

Mevasseret was an important point in the Six Day War. IDF soldiers penetrated the Green Line here, then conquered the village of Biddu. Using this circuitous route they reached Nebi Samuel and eventually Jerusalem.

In 2003 a mid-Second Temple era burial cave with three niches was discovered in Mevasseret. This is deemed to be of not great importance, since similar graves of the period are known elsewhere in the Jerusalem area. The cave was also pilfered, apparently in ancient times.

If you are a beer fan and want to make your own brew, Denny Neilson offers a unique experience. He runs beer making courses in English for both beginners and intermediate students. In two three-hour sessions held one week apart he offers hands-on instruction, with students coming away with a six pack that they brew themselves. Details of the NIS 350 course can be had by calling Denny at 054-638 1102. He is also an excellent source for three varieties of apple cider, all sold from his business in Mevasseret.

Qastel

The Qastel rests on a high hill overlooking the Jerusalem–Tel Aviv Highway. The hill dominates the view of both today's highway and the parallel ancient road to the south. It is, therefore, not surprising that the Romans built a fortress, Castelum Romanum, there to guard the road.

The Crusaders did the same. They built the Belvoir Fortress (one of several with the same or similar name).

In modern times the Qastel played a crucial role in the fight for Jerusalem during the War of Independence.

On the night of April 2, 1948 Jewish forces took possession of the Qastel, but the Arabs were quick to take up the fight. It was clear to both sides that whoever controlled the Qastel determined the access of people and supplies to Jerusalem.

Abdel-Qader al-Husseini (1908–1948), the Arab commander and nephew of the Mufti of Jerusalem, Hajj al-Amin Husseini, was killed in battle on the second day of fighting and was buried after a funeral in Al-Aqsa Mosque.

The Husseini family was prominent in Arab Jerusalem. One of his children was Faisal al-Husseini (1940–2001), who was the PLO representative for Jerusalem

After almost a week of battle the Qastel rested in Jewish hands.

Directions: From Har'el Interchange on the Jerusalem–Tel Aviv Highway (exit to Mevasseret-Zion), drive in the direction of Maoz Zion. Continue past the municipal building and turn right into Rechov Ma'ale Haqastel. Open: April–September: 0800–1700; October-March: 0800–1600. Not Sabbath observant. Fee: Adults NIS12, Children NIS6. Telephone: 02-533-0476.

Motza

For many travelers Motza is best known as the area next to the sharp curve in the highway just before the ascent to Jerusalem. Motza, however, is mentioned twice in the Bible, and very prominently in the Mishna (Succah 4:5) as a source of *aravot* that were used in the Temple.

A decision was taken to straighten the highway with a bypass that was to have been built in 2003 to avoid the curve, the scene of many traffic accidents. The bypass construction, however, was delayed when important archeological remnants were unearthed. It had been known that Motza was the center of extensive farm lands. The first stages of road construction revealed storage rooms demonstrating that Motza was also a warehouse during the late Second Temple period for produce to be brought to Jerusalem.

The name "Motza," is known from an inscription on an eighth century BCE earthenware vessel discovered in northern Jerusalem. Tradition says that the name is related to agriculture. The most popular explanation for the name is a settlement *outside* the Jerusalem royal tax zone (for produce). It was once thought that the reference was Roman, but after the discovery of the vessel it is more plausible that the monarch involved was a king of Judea.

Do not be fooled by today's road that passes through Motza. The curve has been there for centuries, but the highway along its current route dates only to 1942. From Roman times travelers descended from the Qastel on a winding path, then started the two hour trek from the curve to the Old City on a dirt road with a steep incline inside the Jerusalem Forest.

As early as Byzantine times there was a church and pilgrims' hospice in Motza, just before making the last ascent to Jerusalem. Today the foundation of the Byzantine building serves as a catering hall on the floor below a synagogue.

Over the years a new church was built in Motza during the Crusader period by pilgrims who mistakenly thought they had found the valley in which David had confronted Goliath.

It was only in 1860 that Jews returned to Motza. It was considered a daring step when two Jews moved so far from physical protection inside the Old City walls. Members of the Yehudah and Yellin families started acquiring land and water rights in Kolonia for the purpose of farming, but from the very beginning there were problems. Neither was an Ottoman citizen, so they were forbidden by law to purchase land. Five years later cutouts were found, and the lands were officially transferred to Jewish hands.

Yehoshua Yellin (1843–1924) was quick to appreciate business potential. In 1869 the Ottomans began to pave the Jaffa–Jerusalem road for use by buggies. By 1871 Yellin built a second storey above the Byzantine ruins and opened a café and small hotel for travelers who feared they might reach Jerusalem after nightfall, when the city gates were locked. In the other direction there were those who left Jerusalem in the afternoon, stayed overnight in Yellin's hotel, and made an early morning start for Ramla and Jaffa.

Motza boasts of an important "first" in modern Israeli history. In 1880–81 Yellin and a partner opened a short-lived roof-tile factory, the first substantial Jewish industry outside the Old City.

During the Ottoman period Motza was known as Kolonia, a quiet Arab village. In 1929 Arabs from Kolonia participated in the murderous anti-Jewish riots; they slaughtered some of the Jewish residents. The village was evacuated by Arabs in 1948 and leveled in 1955. Portions of several buildings still remain, more as an historical curiosity than important structures.

In the early 1890s Yehoshua Yellin built a house for himself behind the hotel, which he sold. The location was perfect, with a deep well in the courtyard. That residence has recently been under restoration. The story of the hotel took various turns. In the first years of the twentieth century four families shared the building as a residence. In 1917 the Cohen family moved in, and separated rooms for a hotel, school and synagogue. The hotel, though, was a victim of technology, when motor vehicles were introduced in 1922, and it was no longer necessary to rest animals and travelers in Motza. In 1948 the building was used as an earthenware factory. Then in 1961 a noteworthy change took place. Two religious Jews decided to restore the building to its historic use. Once again the hotel with a Byzantine foundation became a synagogue. It was realized that praying in someone's house was not a long-term solution. Since that time the synagogue has been remodeled, and air conditioning has been installed. Shabbat prayers are held there regularly, even though access is not very convenient for most of the local residents.

That, in short, is the history of the small synagogue that sits several meters off the road at the curve in the Jerusalem–Tel Aviv Highway. Even today it is a pleasant stop during what seems a long drive on the highway. Rezoning in the 1990s placed much of Motza within Jerusalem city limits.

Nes Harim

This is a small *moshav* established in 1950 by immigrants from Kurdistan and Morocco. It is located eight kilometers from Jerusalem. The ruins of a Byzantine monastery have been uncovered near the southwest side of the *moshav*. The monastery was decorated with multicolored mosaics. The tradition of wine continues in Nes Harim with the Katlav Winery (see Kosher Wine Guide).

The American Independence Park near Nes Harim, developed in 1976 to commemorate the American bi-centennial, contains the ruins of a Crusader fortress that dominated the road from Emek Ha'ela to Jerusalem. Remains of the fortress, vaults, a wall and towers, tunnels, a columbarium and an olive press were found.

A JNF visitor information center provides pamphlets with historic and general information of the area and its surroundings. Often the information booth has written material but no clerk. This is the starting point for two hiking paths, one easy and short and one strenuous and long. The easy path (paved and wheelchair accessible though hard for the person sitting to push himself) has a rocky landscape, and is a very scenic 1.5 kilometers each way, leading to an impressive observation point; the entrance to the path is to the left of the cafeteria (not kosher). The longer, 2.4 kilometer path, takes about two hours (attesting to its relative difficulty) and leads to the Beit Atav spring and ruins (the subjects of various legends); experienced hikers can continue to Nachal HaMeara. The entrance is to the right of the cafeteria.

Note that the American Independence Park is quite large—thirty thousand dunhams. There are other entrances, various archeological ruins, and numerous picnic opportunities.

Nes Harin - Katlav Winery - See Kosher Wine Guide

Neve Ilan and Kiryat Ye'arim

Neve Ilan, to the east of Kiryat Ye'arim, was established in 1946 as an outpost to help control the Jerusalem–Tel Aviv Highway. Today it is best known as home to a television broadcasting studio. Maaleh Hachamisha is named in memory of five JNF workers who were murdered in the area.

Neve Shalom

This is a village established by Jewish and Palestinian Arabs as a gesture toward peace and understanding. The experiment might be politically appealing, but there is nothing of religious historical interest for the tourists. The hotel and conference center do not have kashrut certification.

Ramat Raziel

This small village was first settled in 1948. It was named after David Raziel (1910–1941), one of the founders of the Irgun. Today it has fewer than 500 residents.

In 1937 Raziel became the Irgun's Commander of Jerusalem District. The following year he was promoted to the rank of Commander-in-Chief. In 1941 he was dispatched with three others to Iraq on behalf of the British army to fight against the al-Gaylani (Rashid Aali al-Gaylani, 1892-1965) pro-Nazi government. Raziel was killed by a bomb dropped from a German aircraft. He was reburied on Mount Herzl in Jerusalem in 1961.

For information on the modern winery see Kosher Wine Guide.

Sataf

This is a popular nature destination maintained by the Jewish National Fund on the eastern side of Mount Eitan. The one thousand dunham reserve was reportedly first inhabited by 4000 BCE when a Chalcolithic agricultural village was established (remnants can be seen on the longer hiking path that begins near the information center). The area was populated during the periods of the Second Temple and the Byzantines, but the first written mention dates only to the Mamluks.

Two springs, Ein Sataf and Ein Bikura empty below into the Sorek riverbed. The Bikura Spring (Arabic, Ein al-Sharkiya) flows out of a not-so-large "tunnel," carved out of the rock. The water spills from the "tunnel" walls into a pool.

Five marked hiking trails of varied difficulty can challenge the eager hiker. They are between two and three kilometers. Another activity is to enter a cave, from which the spring flows, walk through a tunnel, and come out at the far end. There is no lighting, so take along a reliable flashlight.

The Sataf is located along Route 395. Open daylight hours. No entry fee. Public transportation to reach the Sataf is not at all practical,

(above left) Water Pool with Tunnel
(above right) Coming out of the tunnel
(right) Water Pool

since it leaves passengers a considerable hike from the Sataf. It is best to arrive by private car and park at the lower level. Telephone: 02-642-8462

Telshe Stone

Telshe Stone, to the west of Abu Ghosh, started in the 1970s as an orthodox settlement. The original concept was to build a large yeshiva (named after Telshe/Telze in Lithuania) with money donated by Irving Stone (1903–1989). That project began in 1975, however it ran into financial difficulty. Nevertheless, families did move into the area. In 1992–1993 the larger area of which Telshe Stone is a part, was formally incorporated under the name Kiryat Ye'arim.

Opposite Telshe Stone on a short path about 250 feet south of the main highway is a memorial to those who died in the July 6, 1989 terrorist action against the No. 405 bus (see above entry).

Tzuba

Finding Palmach Tzova, a kibbutz no more than a fifteen-minute drive from Jerusalem, can be a challenge. Palmach Tzova is the formal name, but you will not find it on road signs. There it is called Tzuba.

Part of ancient water supply

The kibbutz was founded in October 1948 by two groups of soldiers from the Palmach; one group consisted of sabras primarily from Petach Tikva, and the other immigrant Holocaust survivors. The area had been conquered on July 12–13, 1948 as part of Operation Danny. Hence the first part of the official name—Palmach. Tzova (note spelling) is known from the Biblical books of Samuel and Chronicles; therefore the second part of the name. Why Tzuba (note spelling)? That is just the way it is! In any event, there are sites of interest on the kibbutz.

Cistern

In the first years of the twenty-first century Shimon Gibson excavated a large cistern, discovered in 1999 by Reuven Kalifon. The cistern is quite extensive, however its total size is unknown, since a major section is still filled with mud. It appears to be twenty-four meters long, five meters high, and four-and-a-half meters wide; this is a supposition based on the theoretical removal of the rest of the mud. In view of the size the original hypothesis of a *mikva* was rejected. Archeology cannot answer all questions. One issue not clarified is why the steps leading into the cistern are so unusually wide (at the expense of more water storage).

Entrance to water cistern (Sheina)

Tunnel in water cistern (Sheina)

Carbon 14 testing of the plaster on the walls suggests a date of about 1000 BCE. From that period there are only two other known cisterns of roughly similar size—Beit Shemesh and Beer Sheva, both walled cities. As far as is known, there was no wall around Tzova.

First Temple Era Cistern

Etched drawings on the higher parts of the walls are definitely from a much later date (probably the Middle Ages), suggesting that by then there was a considerable amount of dirt-fill in the ancient cistern.

The large size of the cistern is one of several indications that Tzova was a large city in Biblical times.

Outside the cistern there are pools to collect water and a cave. This is all part of the water system of which the cistern is only part. Another item of interest outside the cistern is a series of eight large stones, apparently of no particular practical use. One archeological theory is that they were part of an earlier idol worshipping cult.

Burial Caves

This burial area, carved in rock and located in today's vineyards, dates to more or less the eighth century BCE (around the time of Hizkiyahu). The method of burial was to place the deceased on one of three stone "beds," waiting for the body to decompose.

Ancient Wine Press

The wine press, excavated by Shimon Gibson in 2011, is unusually large, particularly for being outside the walls of a city. The size with five areas to squeeze grapes and three storage pools makes personal use rather dubious. Sharing the wine or commercial use are distinct possibilities, but archeologists have uncovered no proof.

Remnants of a wall surrounding the "winery" have been unearthed. This was possibly built to delineate the property and to keep out certain animals.

An unusual feature is a millstone partially cut in a large rock, then abandoned. Exact dating is difficult, but archeologists prefer the late Second Temple period. One theory is that work on the millstone was

Ancient winery

abruptly ceased, perhaps due to war. If so, the Bar Kochba period is a distinct possibility given battles in the area and the fact that once expelled from the Judean Hills, Jews were not permitted to return.

The kibbutz is hard to reach by public transportation. Historical sites should be visited with a guide. Call the Tourism Office of the kibbutz to arrange a tour in English or Hebrew. Cost varies according to length. Telephone: 02-534-7000. Not wheelchair accessible.

For information on the modern winery see Kosher Wine Guide.

Yad Kennedy

Yad Kennedy memorializes John Fitzgerald Kennedy (JFK) (1917–1963), the thirty-fifth President of the United States.

The 18.3 meter high memorial, designed by David Resnick, former director of the Israel Architects' Association and architect for the Moshe Castel Museum, is reminiscent of a tree trunk that has been cut, symbolizing a shortened life. A bust of John F. Kennedy is inside together with an eternal flame. The fifty-one columns each contain the emblem of a state and the District of Columbia. The monument was built in 1966 with donations from American Jewish communities.

The memorial is quite out of the way near Moshav Ora and Moshav Aminadav (both established in 1950) on Route 3877. A visit is practical by car only, however the area is quite scenic. Encircling the memorial by foot provides some breath-taking views.

Opposite Moshav Ora at Ein el Hanniya there is a Greek and Roman nymphaeum (monument to water nymphs), which has been reconstructed as best possible after years of neglect and vandalism.

A Yad Kennedy information center operated by the Jewish National Fund is open Sunday–Thursday, 0900–1600; Friday until 1500; Center closed Shabbat. The memorial is always open. Telephone 02-570-9926.

Below the Hills

Beit Shemesh *(See color plate 11, p 101)*

Beit Shemesh has had an erratic history, waffling from a critical geographic crossroads to a town without major importance. It was the city where Philistine settlement came into contact with the Israelites, and it was there that the Philistines returned the *Aron*. Yet, little is known of the city from late-Talmudic until Ottoman times.

The original Beit Shemesh was situated roughly two kilometers south of the railroad tracks that today intersect the north–south highway to the west of the modern city. Excavations in 1911–1912 and again during 1928–1933 yielded a complex view of the past. There was a Bronze Age Canaanite settlement, then an Israelite presence during the period of the Kings. Amongst finding are agricultural implements and nearby burial caves.

The archeological artifacts uncovered, most now housed in the Rockefeller Museum in Jerusalem, speak for themselves. This was no obscure little village. It was an important point on trade routes. Items were found suggesting contact with Cyprus, Egypt, Greece, and probably Assyria. There was also local industry. A furnace to prepare bronze for metalworking was unearthed, as well as two presses to squeeze olive oil. At least eight ancient burial caves have been found (including three that complicated the construction of a new commercial center opposite the city's market place). None of these is open to the public at this time.

Remains of Ancient Bet Shemsh (Sheina)

Contact was not only with far-off countries abroad. Hebrew seals, similar to those from Ramat Rachel, were also uncovered.

A visit to Tel Beit Shemesh is oddly enough not really recommended. The site has not been properly prepared for tourists, and there are no signs properly explaining the excavations. Only a series of unmarked dirt paths provides access to the area. Nor is parking particularly easy. The unpaved parking area is small, and it is difficult to maneuver a car, especially if a second vehicle is parked. Mud after rains is another problem.

Another testimony to the importance of Biblical Beit Shemesh is the graves of prominent personages in the area—Dan, Samson, and Manoach. (The purported grave of Samson in Gaza City has no Jewish authenticity.)

The ancient construction of the city, complicated by the overlay of a Byzantine church and/or monastery with pilgrims' hospice, was impressive. The city consisted of thirty-two dunhams of densely built construction surrounded by a protective wall. Nor were the buildings at all flimsy. They were made of thick solid walls, serving both as a building support and a supplement to outer defenses.

Yet, in the Gemara Yerushalmi, Beit Shemesh is curiously mentioned as a small town—the smallest in the area. Geo-politics had obviously changed, and Beit Shemesh lost its strategic importance.

The next significant emergence of Beit Shemesh is during the Ottoman period, when a town sprung up in 1895 on Har Tuv, an area about three kilometers north of the Biblical city, which by then was little more than a neglected *tel.* Har Tuv had residences and industry, and it served as a hub for the numerous villages in the surrounding area. An indication of its importance was the Har Tuv station on the Ottoman railroad from the Lydda interchange to Jerusalem. The railroad had the effect of spurring further development.

The 1948 War of Independence changed the face of the area. Fleeing Arabs destroyed Har Tuv. The Arab village of Beit Jit, just off today's road from Shimshon Junction to Ramla, was captured by Jewish forces. It became the Har'el Outpost on the makeshift Burma Road (see entry below).

As 1948 fighting eased, the road from Shimshon Junction to Nachshon Junction was completed, and on December 7, 1948 Israeli Prime Minister David Ben Gurion (1886-1973) inaugurated it as the "Road of Heroism." It joined the segment from Nachshon Junction to Ramla and became part of the new main Jerusalem–Tel Aviv Highway, in use as such until after the Six Day War.

Then came the *ma'abarot*, the temporary camps used to house immigrants. More than three thousand were housed on Har Tuv. From adversity, however, came seeds for the future. On December 6, 1950 the current municipality of Beit Shemesh (incorporated with full city status in 1991) was founded, and residents began to move in. Slowly, the *ma'abarot* were taken down, and the residents were transferred to permanent housing.

1. Museum at Masada *(See p. 15)*

2. From the Synagogue in Jericho *(See p. 27)*

3. From a synagogue in Gaza *(See p. 28)*

4. Inside the Boyan Synagogue *(See p. 29)*

5. Inside the Karlin Synagogue *(See p. 29)*

6. (above left) Art in wood
(See p. 46)

7. (above right) Art in wood
(See p. 46)

8. (left) A commercial bakery at home offering a different gift *(See p. 50)*

9. (right) Products of a home industry © *(See p. 50)*

10. (below) Family Dinner in Safed (Tsefat) © *(See p. 63)*

11. (above) Hiking path near Bet Shemesh (Sheina)
(See p. 95)

12. (left) Air Force Memorial
(See p. 117)

13. View of the Ayala valley *(See p. 117)*

14. Replica of Tel Aviv at Mini Israel Museum *(See p. 119)*

15. Replica of Tel of Rachel's Tomb at Mini Israel Museum *(See p. 119)*

16. Typical hiking path sign *(See p. 123)*

17. Wadi Qelt *(See p. 123)*

18. Restaurant in Itamar. All dairy products made with goats milk (Sheina) *(See p. 132)*

19. Olives from Shilo. Another local industry with tours available (Sheina) *(See p. 137)*

20. Courtesy of Ruth's vineyard © *(See p. 158)*

21. (left) A winery that became kosher
(See p. 159)

22. (below) Domaine du Castel Winery
(See p. 161)

23. (above) Rabbinical supervisor in the winery
(See p. 163)

24. (right) Author Dr. Levinson with Mr. Teperberg, the owner of Teperberg Winery (Sheina)
(See p. 163)

25. (left) Wine made by Tzor'a. All grapes are from Neve Ilan *(See p. 166)*

26. (below) Wine tasting at Tzor'a *(See p. 166)*

27. At Mony checking the hecsher on the bottle *(See p. 167)*

28. Mony's vineyard *(See p. 167)*

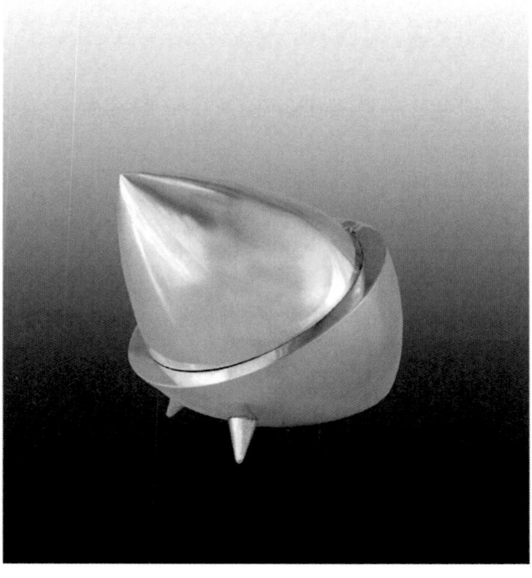

29. (above) P'sagot visitors center at the winery *(See p. 172)*

30. (left) Etrog box © Courtesy of Yossi Matityahu Contemporary Designs, 8 King David Street, Jerusalem)

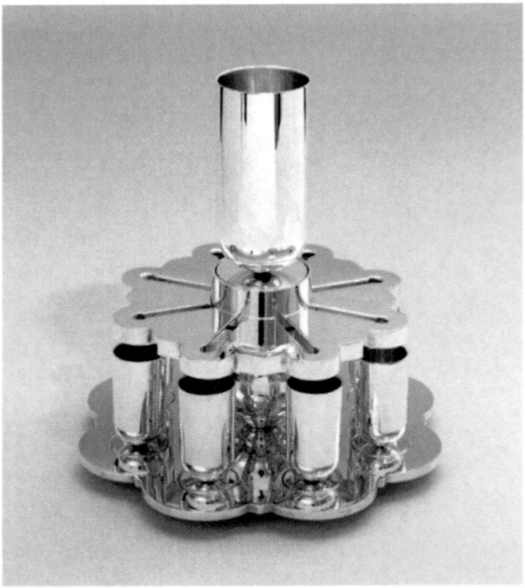

31. (above) Honey dish. (© Courtesy of Yossi Matityahu Contemporary Designs, 8 King David Street, Jerusalem)

32 (right) Wine fountain. Wine has also made its way into modern Judaica art. (© Courtesy of Yossi Matityahu Contemporary Designs, 8 King David Street, Jerusalem)

In the 1950s and 1960s Shimshon Junction was an important stop for all buses between Jerusalem and Tel Aviv, but again the importance of Beit Shemesh faded. First, after the 1967 Six Day War the Latrun Junction was opened to car traffic; then buses were allowed; and finally, the modern highway was inaugurated between Latrun and Sha'ar HaGay. Eventually, the railroad fell into disuse, until attempts were made to revitalize it during the past few years. Beit Shemesh stopped being a major transit station.

Ramat Beit Shemesh

In the Ashkenazi and ultra-orthodox worlds, modern Beit Shemesh is best known for Ramat Beit Shemesh Alef and Bet, religious neighborhoods both started in the 1990s, and for the older Scheinfeld neighborhood of the city.

The ancient history of Ramat Beit Shemesh is beginning to be discovered. Recent archeological digs have uncovered remains dating to the First Temple era. A *mikva* and an olive press have been unearthed from the Hasmonean and Roman periods. It seems that Ramat Beit Shemesh of today was agricultural with an economy based upon grapes and olives. One of the difficulties in resurrecting the past is that the Byzantines destroyed much of the area, again for agricultural purpose. They broke down older buildings and reused the stones to build terraces.

Burma Road

The Burma Road is a dirt "thoroughfare" from Nachos to Beit Meir, circumventing segments of the Tel Aviv to Jerusalem highway that had fallen into Arab hands during the War of Independence. Reconnaissance took place on the night of May 30, 1948, after the fall of Beit Jit to Arab forces. Even from the onset it was recognized that building a road through the mountains would be difficult, but it was judged to be possible. Work began. Opened on the night of June 10–11, 1948, the Burma Road (named after the World War II connection from Burma to China) helped maintain contact with Jerusalem.

Jerusalem had been under siege periodically from the UN declaration of partition on November 29, 1947. The last large convoy succeeded in reaching Jerusalem in April 1948. By the time the British left Palestine, the Arab Legion had captured the area of the Latrun Monastery (established in 1890 and still in operation) and the police Tegart (see entry below) building that controlled the road to Jerusalem.

Watchtower on the Burma Road (Sheina)

Remains of Ancient Bet Shemsh (Sheina)

Israeli attempts to capture Arab positions failed, so it was decided to outflank them by building an alternative route safe from sniper and canon fire. Initial trips were problematic with overturned vehicles and others that had to be pushed, but by mid-June even the pot-holes were repaired. Eventually, fuel and water lines were also placed along the "highway."

The Har'el Outpost near Beit Shemesh provides a panoramic view of the surrounding area, but it is blocked by trees. The military vantage point was from a watch tower, entrance to which is not permitted today. Yet, the Outpost is a pleasant stop amidst a sizeable JNF forest. There are picnic tables, bathrooms, ample parking, and well-marked signs explaining the Burma Road and its route. For the adventurous, there is a ten kilometer hiking path from the Shimshon–Ramla Road to Shaar HaGay.

Emek Ha'ela

Along Route 38 is the Emek Ha'ela, where David fought Goliath (I Samuel 17); it is also the site of the slaughter of thirty-five people in a caravan to Gush Etzion in 1948 (probably on a hilltop on the Israeli side of the former cease fire line with Jordan). (See the Kfar Etzion entry.) A mountain with climbing (part of the Israel Trail)/driving route provides an impressive overview of the area.

The southern segment of the seven kilometer valley is to be covered in another volume in this series. See Kosher Wine Guide.

Industrial Zone

Gilro Ice Cream Cones

Surviving the Holocaust was a daunting challenge, but the fight to survive did not end with liberation. For many survivors the effort to return to normalcy and build a future meant new problems and uncertainty. Avraham Gelbard lived to look back on what he had seen in Auschwitz. For the most part it was too horrific to relate. He tried to suppress his memories. Even years later he spoke very little about this period in his life. Most of his family had been murdered during the years of Nazi rule.

After liberation Gelbard realized that life had to start anew. He had to look to the future and rebuild his existence. He returned to his native Zagłębie in Poland and re-established himself in the bakery business, but things went wrong very quickly. Gelbard's brother was murdered by Poles. This was not the place to stay. He moved to Stuttgart, but Germany was also not an answer. Gelbard had family who immigrated to

Israel before the War. Israel was his next stop. The question then became one of earning a livelihood.

Gelbard was a baker by trade. What was missing in Israel? Ice cream cones with no kashrut problems! In 1950 he teamed up with his brother-in-law and started the Gilro Company, making ice cream cones in Jerusalem's Romema District.

Gilro's cones were a success, but the market was changing with time. Gelbard passed away, and his son, Avi, took over. The factory in Romema became far too small, so in the late 1980s the company moved to a much larger facility with modern equipment in Beit Shemesh. The brand was the called Alma (the name of Avi's daughter) as a part of image change. There are no factory tours at this time.

Papou-Chips (Chips-li)

Little did Michael Papoushado, an Israeli studying law in England, know that a taste of a potato chip in Newcastle would change his entire life. In the early 1990s Papoushado went into a deli and decided to purchase a bag of hand-made potato chips rather than the usual machine made type. They were more expensive, but curiosity reigned. The cashier rung up the sale. They were great! They were crispy and had the taste of potatoes, not salt. Papoushado and his friends finished off the £ 1 bag in five minutes.

As time went by, Papoushado left the world of law and lawyers. He could not forget the taste of the potato chip! He worked for a pretzel company. He worked in his father's condiments factory (Eida hashgocho) in Holon. He learned the business of snack food, then he staked out his own future. He found a suitable facility in Beit Shemesh where he wanted to start his own business — hand-made potato chips. There was no Israeli competition.

Starting manufacture is much easier said than done. One major hurdle is equipment. Papoushado's budget did not allow him to purchase brand new equipment, so he searched high and low for something second hand. Finally, he found something and raced off to Virginia to beat other buyers. Papoushado bought both equipment and know-how, but not the know-how to put his newly acquired equipment into working order. For that he needed his own resources. When everything was ready the seller came to Israel to teach his expertise.

Papoushado has a sound business sense. He realized that he would be making mistakes, so he started small. He tried this. He tried that. Now his company cannot meet the orders that keep coming in.

How good are the Chips-li potato chips? This author gave chips to numerous people, adults and children. Yes, there are those who prefer the popular brands. Most tasters, however, were like Papoushado in Newcastle. They preferred Chips-li. As several people said, "The taste grows on you."

Eshtaol

Spice Farm

Behind the winery there is a pleasant surprise—a 300 square meter store opened in 2006 and specializing in all kinds of spices from exotic tea blends to cinnamon soap. With advance notice a twenty to twenty-five minute lecture about spices and their use can be arranged without charge for groups. Then tourists are welcome to walk through the store. Individuals are also invited to shop, and explanations can be given when staff is available. Gift packages with various products are also on sale. All house label products are under rabbinical supervision.

From Route 38 turn northward in the direction of Tzuba at the Eshtaol Junction, then make the first left down a poorly paved road. Telephone: 02-992-4995/6.

Latrun

IDF Armored Corps Museum
(See color plate 12, p 101)

The Latrun section of the Ayala Valley, midway between Jerusalem and Ramla, is a critical point controlling the road between the coast and the Judean Hills. *(See color plate 13, p 102)* The British understood that strategic importance, and after the riots of 1936–1939 they constructed a police station in standard Charles Tegart (1881–1946) architecture to secure the area.

Armored vehicles at the museum in Latrun (Sheina)

Typical Tegart architecture

Tegart, himself, was considered a very competent policeman, but with a strong inclination to torturing those interrogated. He improved the crime situation in India, where he spent most of his career. In 1938 he was transferred to Palestine. He is perhaps best known for more than three dozen Mandate police stations of various sizes, the design of which still bears his name. The basic architectural plan was approved in 1938.

Brown walls surround a central courtyard, and there is often an elevated watchtower. Most of these Tegart buildings are still in use today both in Israel and in the Palestinian Authority.

The Latrun building had decisive importance in the War of Independence, when it was occupied by the Arab Legion after British withdrawal. Twice Jewish forces attacked the building. Twice they were repelled. Only in 1967 was the Tegart building conquered by the IDF.

In the late 1980s the Latrun Tegart building and its surrounding area became the IDF Armored Corps Museum. There one will find an impressive collection of some 150 armored vehicles, both in the service of the IDF over the years and those captured from enemy forces. There is also a wall of names of those in the Armored Corps who fell as result of enemy action, and a motivational film explaining the Corps.

In addition to regular tours, there is an explanatory pamphlet available in English and Hebrew versions, and a guided tour accessible by cell phone (050-800-0222. Visitors must have their own cell phones, and air time is charged).

The museum is open to the public Sunday through Thursday 0830–1700, Friday 0830–1400. Tours in English can be arranged by calling

08-925-5268. Entrance fee: Adults NIS30, Children and seniors NIS20. Not Sabbath observant.

Park Canada (Ayalon)

This park is the dream of Bernard Bloomfield of Montréal, a former president of JNF Canada, who led a fundraising campaign to raise $15 million to establish the recreational area. The park was ceremonially opened by former Canadian Prime Minister John Diefenbaker (1895-1979) and completed in 1975.

Jewish settlement goes back to Biblical times, and it is known from Joshua 19:42 that the territory belongs to the Tribe of Dan.

In the park one can visit the ruins of Emmaus, the site of a Hasmonean battle and an ancient city whose remnants can still be seen—a Roman bathhouse, a Hasmonean cemetery, and a wine press. One can also see two late-Roman aqueducts, and the remains of a Crusader fortress (Castellum Arnaldi).

The Burma Road, mentioned elsewhere in this book, is best known as an Israeli attempt to reach Jerusalem by circumventing Arab forces, but there was also another "Burma" Road that passed through today's park (see entry).

Mini-Israel *(See color plates 14 & 15, p 102 & 103)*

Mini-Israel is a miniature of Israel in every sense, from Mount Hermon and the Golan in the north to Eilat in the south. This bird's-eye view of Israel was the dream of three Israelis on a typical post-army trip in the late 1980s. They saw a miniature village in Madurodam in the Netherlands and decided they would build something bigger and better. They did. On seventy dunhams of land leased from Kibbutz Nachshon near Latrun, they built the world's largest miniature village with four hundred buildings including twenty-two synagogues (all made from polyester, coated with polyurethane and painted with weatherproof automotive paint) and thousands of people, most constructed on a scale of 1:25. Not everything stands still. Sixty-five kilometers of chains make people move, cars travel, and airplanes position themselves on the airfield.

The seventeen thousand dwarf trees in the exhibit are grown by the bonsai method and are cared for by a staff of six gardeners. Plastic would mean much less care, but natural plants add significantly to the realism of the exhibit. To deal with the seventy thousand total plants there are five thousand kilometers of irrigation pipes in a fully automated and computerized system.

The key to maximizing on a visit to Mini-Israel is the guide. Each exhibit has its own story. It is not enough to marvel at the exactness of the miniatures. It is fascinating to hear why the Hadera power plant was named after Yitzchak Rabin, and how the IDF established its headquarters in Tel Aviv's old Sharona district.

An English/Hebrew recorded tour is being installed, and the park is working on a special version for religiously observant visitors.

Over the years the clock in Yafo has become a symbol of the city. When showing the miniature the guide explains that the French presented six clocks to the Ottomans in celebration of the jubilee of Sultan Abdul-Hamid II. Cynics say that this was the polite French message to the Ottomans that the time of their crumbling Empire was passing.

The replica of the Great Synagogue of Tel Aviv, erected in 1926 on Rechov Allenby, is truly impressive. The building is surrounded by a series of large pillars. Why? Of course! To hold up the huge and heavy dome that dominates the structure.

A renowned landmark at the southeastern entrance to Bnei Braq is the Coca Cola bottling plant. Even the adjacent intersection is informally named after the soda company. Coca Cola honored the Arab boycott until 1968, when it started operations in Israel. The company has no regrets. Today, according to the Mini-Israel guide, the Bnei Braq plant is one of the company's ten largest and produces one million bottles of soft drinks every day.

Not everything in Israel is buildings, either modern or ancient. Mini-Israel also has a "typical kibbutz." After all, for many years the kibbutz was a landmark of Israel, and it still is the home of many Israeli cows. Those cows produce on average fourteen thousand liters of milk each year, twice as much as in Europe.

Another miniature in Mini-Israel is Masada and Herod's palace (see entry above). For centuries Masada was a well-entrenched legend in Jewish lore based upon the writings of Josephus. Was it true? No one knew for sure. The site was identified in 1842, but the first serious archeological excavations commenced in 1963. Then came the electrifying news. The story of Masada was true. It was the last stronghold of the Zealots who held out against the Romans for three years after the fall of Jerusalem, then took their own lives rather than being captured. A highlight of the miniature recreation is the Zealot synagogue, the original of which dates back to the Second Temple era. (See Masada entry in this book)

Thirty-five percent of Mini-Israel is devoted to Jerusalem—disproportionate in terms of geographic size but not in terms of importance.

The Western Wall is represented, as are the excavations at the Southern Wall to the Temple Mount. There is even a replica of Shaar HaRachamim on the Eastern Wall. (No, do not look for the Northern Wall; it was destroyed centuries ago and replaced by a wall that encloses an expansion to the Temple Mount.

It's all there—the King David Hotel, the Jewish Agency, and even the Amphitheatre on Mount Scopus. Not everything, however, is up-to-date. The lone arch atop the Churva Synagogue in the Jewish Quarter is still depicted, even though the synagogue has been reconstructed and includes a complete dome, modeled after the one that was destroyed in 1948.

Not every miniature in Mini-Israel is a replica of something that exists. There is one blatant exception. The Egged Bus Company donated the drawings for a bus museum which they hope to build in the near future, but which does not yet exist. The miniature of that museum is on display.

There are many reasons to visit Mini-Israel. It can be a fine introduction to Israel before you see the country, a quiz to find out what you think you recognize, or a pleasant review exercise after a tour of Israel.

Visits in inclement weather are not recommended, since the facility is outdoors.

Entrance fees are adults NIS69, seniors NIS59, children 2–5 NIS15. The park opens at 1000. Not Sabbath observant. Closing depends upon the season. Information about specific hours can be obtained by calling 08-913-0000. Group reservations and discounts are available by calling 08-913-0010. Note that public transportation is impractical to reach Mini-Israel. Discounted taxi service is available by calling in advance.

The restaurant at Mini-Israel does not have supervision. A separate Sabbath observant kitchen under rabbinic supervision can be opened for groups.

Sha'alvim

This religious kibbutz was founded in 1951 and called after a name that appears in Joshua 19:42, Judges 1:35 and in I Kings 4:9. The yeshiva, for which the kibbutz is well known, began in 1961.

The kibbutz is located on the remains of a depopulated Arab village, Salbit (estimated 572 residents in 1948). In quiet diplomacy during the War of Independence Israeli forces promised not to attack the village if the nearby water pipeline to Jerusalem would not be destroyed. Despite the agreement, Arabs detonated the pipeline (remains can be seen off the road between the Latrun Museum and Mini-Israel). Israel then captured the village.

Vineyard Adventure

For several weeks during the summer the kibbutz runs a special outdoor program including picking of grapes and treading to make juice, arts and crafts, uses of straw, and producing herbal tea.

Admission for children two years and older is NIS35 (NIS30 a child from the third child in a family). Adults from age fourteen years NIS20. Telephone: 08-925-9205 or 050-202-2698.

Tzor'a

Tzor'a is a kibbutz founded in December, 1948 as part of a program to populate key areas. The name is based upon a verse in Judges 13:25. It is quite possible that the site might have been a Canaanite city, Zorah. An ancient wine press has been found in Tzor'a.

The Jewish National Fund has organized a ten kilometer driving route that starts near Tzor'a and includes the Biblical site where Samson is thought to have been born, burial graves, and water sources. There are also numerous statues along the way.

For modern wineries, see Kosher Wine Guide.

To the North from Jerusalem

Anatot

Sometimes a mistake is made, and it is virtually impossible to correct. Try following the signs to Anatot, a mostly secular settlement just outside Pisgat Zeev in northern Jerusalem. There are no signs! Well, there are signs, but they all say Almon.

Modern Anatot was founded in 1982 with its appellation based on Jeremiah 1:1, however the name was soon changed to Almon after geographers realized that the biblical home of Jeremiah was at a different, albeit nearby location, probably in Khirbet As-Sid. Modern Anatot was, in fact, on the site of Biblical Almon (Joshua 21:18) near the Arab village of Anata. (There are symbolic remains just past the guard station at the entrance to the settlement.) Today Almon has a population of 220 families, and even many of them still call it Anatot. The name stuck.

Anatot (excuse me for the inaccuracy) has no heavy industry, but it does have several sites of a different nature that make a visit memorable.

Winery – See Kosher Wine Guide

Nachal Prat / Wadi Qelt (see plates 16 & 17 p 103, 104)

An unforgettable sight is Wadi Qelt, the popular name in Arabic for the Hebrew Nahal Prat, which flows for twenty-eight kilometers. It is a nature reserve set up in 2002 and a popular valley for hiking in the Judean Desert. The *wadi* with its three water sources provides an opportunity to see hyraxes and gazelles in the wild. There are also riparian and aquatic plants, including watercress, pennyroyal, toad rush, clammy inula, oleander, narrow-leaved reedmace and common reeds.

A marked hiking path begins in the Almon (Anatot) settlement and descends to the *wadi*. There are two other marked paths in the area. The long path takes about nine hours, must be undertaken only in groups, and has to be coordinated with the Israeli Army (Tel. 02-530-5511 or 5372).

For the less adventurous, cars can travel a narrow and dangerously winding road from the access to Almon (Anatot) and ending in a parking area next to a Mandate-era pumping station, now converted into a Visitors'

Center/Gift Shop with bathroom facilities. Nearby are picnic tables. A short walk can be taken along the stream with picturesque views of water flowing between the rocks. There are also vestiges of several aqueducts, one dating to the Hasmonean period. Bronze Age remnants were found in excavations conducted in 1968. In the *wadi* there are also the remains of other pumping stations that provided water to Jerusalem until 1970.

The winter palaces of Hasmonean kings are further into the *wadi*. One of the palaces was discovered by Ehud Netzer (1934–2010), who estimated that it dates from between 70 and 50 BCE, and was purportedly destroyed by an earthquake in 31 BCE. The working theory is that Herod built a palace on part of the remains. The synagogue includes a *mikva*, a small courtyard with seven or eight rooms, and main hall with seating for almost seventy people.

In more recent years a very strange incident took place in Wadi Qelt. Toward the end of World War II the Germans in collusion with Hajj Al-Amin Husseini, plotted to poison the drinking water of Tel Aviv. They landed or parachuted five operatives near Jericho, and the group found an initial hiding place in the caves of Wadi Qelt. Mandate authorities were alerted by Bedouins, who had discovered gold coins, which were supposed to finance the group. Fortunately, this led to the foiling of the plot.

Fees to Wadi Qelt are paid at the entrance in Anatot. Adults NIS20. Children (5–18) NIS9. Israeli senior citizens and disabled NIS10. Hours: 0800–1600 (1700 in summer) except Friday and Holiday eves closing one hour earlier. Telephone: 02-654-1255. Pamphlets with a map and instructions are available in Hebrew and English. Note: The nature reserve is extremely crowded during Chol HaMoed, vacation periods and Israel Independence Day.

Biblical Museum

In the early 1980s Abraham Noham decided that after a career in education, he would dedicate his efforts to art. He started working in wood, then devoted his efforts to oil paintings on canvas. His themes are the biblical experience and aspects of Jewish history. This is not a typical museum or art gallery; it is the collection of the artist displayed in his home. The paintings are meant to convey a message. They are not for sale.

As Noham explains, "The Bible is not a myth. It is truth.... I try to show what there is in the Bible." It is in that vein that he paints. One picture, for example, shows the travels of Abraham from Ur Casdim to Haran, then onward to Canaan. In another two paintings he depicts Goliath as a giant constructed from imposing rigid blocks.

Not surprisingly, there is a painting showing the Sabbath as the center of Jewish life. In a tour of his work Noham related that an innovation of Judaism was a Divine decree of the Sabbath, rather than a day of rest dictated by a mortal king.

Visiting the "museum" is certainly a captivating experience. There is no entrance fee, and hours are by prior arrangement. Telephone: 02-586-0333.

Petting Zoo

This is a small petting zoo designed for children to enjoy animals. The zoo is open on Tuesday, Thursday, and Friday mornings by arrangement. Telephone: 02-571-2150. No charge.

Pony Rides

There is a ranch area where pony rides can be arranged by appointment. Call 02-586-8880 or 050-557-6035.

Ariel

Ariel, founded in 1978, is located 40 kilometers east of Tel Aviv, and 60 kilometers north of Jerusalem. The city can be reached conveniently from both Jerusalem and Tel Aviv. The Ariel University Center was established in 1982.

Holocaust and Heroism Memorial

There is a Holocaust and Heroism Museum primarily highlighting artwork that tries to explain what happened during the Nazi period.

The museum is located at Rechov Nachshonim 44. Entrance is free. For hours and to arrange tours call 03-906-0105.

Eshel HaShomron

The Garden of Biblical Samaria in Eshel HaShomron was established in 2001. It contains a series of biblical models. It is located along Route 6. Telephone: 03-936-6841. Located at Eshel Hashomron Hotel Ariel, Post Office Box 1822, Ariel 44837.

Ariel Industrial Zone

The Ariel Industrial Zone was approved in 1998. It is on Route 5, near the Barkan Industrial Park. It is about seventeen kilometers over the Green Line. The zone employs almost two thousand workers.

Achva: An Introduction to Techina and Halva

The year 1929 is often remembered for the riots of Hebron, and for the onset of the Great Depression. Yet daily life continued. Netanya was founded. Tel Aviv was a small but growing town. The *yishuv* continued to expand as Jews immigrated from abroad. In a small store in Tel Aviv four immigrants—an unlikely combination from Greece, Turkey, Poland and Russia—started a business, Achdut. There was no Jewish manufacturer of halva in Palestine, except for a very small operation on Queen Mary Street (today Sholomziyon Hamalka) in Jerusalem. The Tel Aviv group wanted to fill the gap.

Success was immediate, and several years later three families united to form another Jewish company, Achva, that produced halva and candy.

Making Techina and Halva ©

The competitors were located on the same street in Tel Aviv. Not long afterwards the two companies combined. In 1947 another halva manufacturer opened in the Jewish Quarter in Jerusalem, only to relocate to Machne Yehuda due to the 1948 fighting. Today that latter company has two stores in the marketplace.

What is halva? In many areas halva is made from a mixture of flour, oil, and sweetener, often containing nuts or raisins. The India-Pakistan area has a variety based on pumpkin seeds. At least one Turkish company adds sunflower seeds. The halva more familiar to Israel is 50 percent sesame seeds (tachina) mixed with 50 percent sugars and no oil added. The sesame seeds themselves are rather oily.

Not all sesame seeds are the same. Originally, Achdut and Achva bought seeds grown in Ekron, near Rechovot, but the Arabs realized the large and oily seeds were inferior; it was therefore common for Arab companies to import sesame from Damascus. Even Achva bought sesame seeds from "abroad." In pre-1948 days one of the partners would travel by train to Damascus and Lebanon, then come back a couple of days later with bags of seeds. Today Achva brings in seeds of the *humera* species from Ethiopia. Arab countries also import the *dares* species from the Sudan. Manufacturers in the Western Hemisphere use sesame from Paraguay, Bolivia, Venezuela and Mexico. These days Joyva, an American company, uses sesame seeds grown in Texas and Oklahoma. In earlier days they imported crops from Guatemala.

Not all sesame seeds, however, can be used for halva. Those sprinkled on bread tend to have less taste and are of a type common to the Indian sub-continent. One tip: if halva contains a high sodium level, that is often an indication that salt was added to blur the mixing of different types (and qualities) of sesame seeds, such as *humera, gonder* and *wellegal wollega* species.

Even in Israel, however, the halva recipe has undergone change. Originally, the sugars were 80 percent sugar and 20 percent glucose (more expensive than sugar). With new technology Achva has been able to reverse those proportions, yielding a healthier product. Not every company is the same. Low quality halva uses only sugar. Al Qaria Al Arabiain Jordan prefers a different recipe; for sweeteners they use 50 percent glucose and 50 percent sugar. Even given modern methods, the preferred method of mixing techina and sweeteners is by hand, using a large stirring utensil in a huge pot.

The Achva product contains no flour, and some of the run is certified for Passover for those who eat *kitniyot*. A sugar-free version substitutes artificial sweetener, but by no means should this be considered "light" or "diet," because of the large amount of natural sesame oil (47 percent in Achva to 60 percent in certain other companies).

In addition to the question of *chametz* there is no doubt that techina and its frequent end-product, halva, need proper rabbinic supervision. There must be certification of no improper additives (Israeli halva often does include cacao and/or pistachios). Sometimes there is bug infestation from storage at the port. Rabbinic supervision approves the two-step straining process which removes extraneous materials such as pebbles as well as insects. Several foreign manufacturers use their machinery for other products as well, including such unrelated items as grape jelly. For the record, the Shomron Rabbinate posts a full time supervisor in Achva; the Eida coordinates with him and sends its own representative once or twice each day.

Halva is sold in numerous shapes and sizes, which of course have no bearing on taste. The most commonly sold in Israel is in the shape of a crescent. Why? As the export manager of Achva has explained, that is traditionally the easiest to place on a slice of bread for a sandwich!

Over the years Achva has grown in size, and in 1997 the company moved from Tel Aviv to a newly built facility in Barkan, yet now even that building is getting too small. Part of the company is in nearby Ariel, where the Barkan contingent is scheduled to relocate. The product line is also expanding. In 1998 Achva introduced organic techina, also from *humera* seeds grown in Ethiopia. This was part of the program to respond to an increasing demand for healthier products. In the same vein, the production of full grain techina began in 2001. Halva is made from regular techina; only organic halva contains full grain techina. The company has also widened its international marketing, including England and continental Europe.

If you like techina in your pita with falafel, do not expect Achva. As the company's CEO explains, restaurants work on price, whereas Achva concentrates on quality. They cannot compete in the industrial market. For similar reason, although Achva went into the pastry business in 2002, they do not market rugelach filled with halva. They have yet to master mass production of a quality product.

There are no tours for the public at this time, nor is there a company store on the factory premises, but the company's products are readily available throughout Israel.

Barkan

This secular settlement was established in 1981. To the east of Barkan there is evidence of Jewish residents in the First and Second Temple periods. The industrial park of Barkan employs some five thousand workers, the vast majority of whom are Arab.

In recent years at least two large companies have left Barkan ostensibly for industrial reasons. One of the companies, a winery, is still called Barkan, even though it moved out of the area. According to some sources the reason for leaving is related to the boycott abroad of goods produced beyond the Green Line.

Beit El

The Arab village of Beitin, seventeen kilometers north of Jerusalem, is the probable site of Biblical Beit El. Right nearby is modern Beit El, a dynamic *yishuv* that was founded in 1977. At first settlers lived in an army base; today, though, Beit El is home to 5,300 residents and a widely known modern orthodox yeshiva.

Beit El was a key city in the pre-Biblical and Biblical periods, in major part due to its geography. Topographically it is part of the central mountain range of Eretz Yisrael. Mountains to the south drain north-south in times of rain; beginning in Beit El they drain east-west, with significant implications for agriculture.

Ancient Beit El

Settlement in ancient Beit El dates back to the Early Bronze Age, when the Canaanites maintained a temple, apparently for sacrificial worship. Excavations reveal that during the Middle Bronze Age there was also idol worship apparently connected with Hathor, an Egyptian female deity of joy, love, and motherhood. In about 1550 BCE Egyptian forces started a 150–200 year occupation of the area. In 1950 archeologists unearthed flint tools and pottery, which assisted in the dating.

Beit El has had a varied history. It is the site of Yaakov Avinu's (Jacob's) dream, as the Torah describes in Genesis 28. The exact site of the ladder has no documented authenticity nor long-term tradition, but it is quite possibly outside the Canaanite city (see Rashi's reference to wild animals, 28:11; see also 35:8 and Rashi, where an area on the outskirts of Beit El is still called Beit El).

The site suggested by many is today next to the remnants of a Byzantine religious structure, which was essentially destroyed in the late twelfth century. Much later a Moslem site (Qabr Ash-sheikh Abdullah, also called Nabi Yaaqub) was built virtually on the same spot.

Where did Jacob gather stones that became one upon which he rested? Adjacent to the religious structures there is a large conglomerate rock clearly comprised of smaller stones. Again, there is no proof, but it is food for thought.

Ancient wine press

The city prospered during the period of the First Temple in Jerusalem, but not all is positive. The city is situated near the dividing line between Judea and the Northern Kingdom; the southern sacrificial altar of Jehoram was in Beit El (a nearby site roughly ten by fifteen *amot*, similar to Shilo) has been suggested as a possible location), and the northern one in Dan.

There is another suggestion of prosperity. Clay tablets dating to the eighth century BCE suggest trade with southern Arabia.

Near Beit El the forces of Judah the Maccabee escaped

from Modi'in; and, the Hasmonean leader ultimately met his demise here in battle. Beit El was conquered by Vespasian in 68 CE, after the fall of Jerusalem. Two indications of the size and importance of Beit El are the Roman decision to station a military garrison there, and the need to build cisterns to augment the natural springs nearby. These cisterns were expanded during the Byzantine period.

Beit El has been excavated several times in the twentieth century, but not all of the excavations were professional in modern terms, and the site and its findings were never prepared properly for tourists. This is particularly evident at the opposite end of the settlement, where the remnants of part of the ancient city have been unearthed, but as of this writing there are no explicatory signs, even though excavations were conducted almost ten years ago.

A good start for a visit is to climb the water tower built in the late 1990s at the edge of the city. The tower provides a panoramic vantage point from which one can see the Land of Israel from Mount Hermon to Tel Aviv and Ashdod on a clear day. Annotated maps highlight the various points, including several of Biblical interest.

In addition to visiting the area associated with Jacob's dream, there is an ancient burial cave and an olive oil production center, with remnants from three or four levels of sophistication, one built next to another. The most primitive method of producing olive oil was to place weight upon the olives or trample upon them. The next historical development was to roll a wheel over the olives in a circular motion (pulled either by manpower or by an animal). Much later weights were placed on wooden boards to squeeze the olives and extract the oil.

For better perspective about Beit El, try the Cultural Center, where a timeline of the ancient city and modern renewal has been affixed to an auditorium wall. A movie (Hebrew, English) is also available, introducing the city. Be prepared for a very unexpected ending!

In addition, there is a marked hiking path that runs through Beit El starting at the winery.

For a tour of Beit El (Hebrew, English), call the Tourism Coordinator at 054-666-8257. A modest fee is charged. A tour of the local tefillin factory is separate; a fee of NIS350 per group is charged, unless tefillin are purchased. Tel. 02-997-5158.

De'ir Dibwan

After Joshua conquered the city of Jericho, he laid siege to Ha-Ai, only to lose the battle because Achan had taken forbidden booty from the previous victory at Jericho. Joshua's forces succeeded in capturing the city after Achan was found out and stoned.

De'ir Dibwan, three kilometers from Beit El, has been identified as one of the possible sites of Ha-Ai. Excavations have revealed a fortified Canaanite city protected by a wall and four watchtowers.

The site is in the Palestine Authority. A visit is not recommended for security reasons.

Itamar

Looking for a very different experience? Itamar, a settlement of 100 families in the Northern Shomron near Shechem, can be an excellent option for a two or three hour visit.

The modern settlement, founded in 1984, is named after the youngest son of Aharon HaCohen (Exodus 6:23), who, according to tradition, is buried nearby. From a small cluster of caravans, today Itamar has expanded into an area of over ten square kilometers.

Givat Olam *(See color plate 18, p 105)*

The highlight of a visit is an unusual restaurant at the far end of Itamar. The rather rustic facility is under the *mehadrin* kashrut supervision of the Shomron rabbinate and many of the products used bear the label of the Eida.

The story of the restaurant starts with Abraham ("Avri") Ran, who saw agricultural production as a method to expand Itamar. Israel certainly has a large number of farms, so he sought a unique niche in the market. The land had not been cultivated for centuries, long before the advent of modern chemical fertilizers. So, Avri made a decision—he would specialize in organic food. As time passed, an industry was established that now accounts for the production of 80 percent of the organic chicken eggs marketed by Tnuva and a very large percentage of the goat milk in Israel. Organic vegetables, strawberries and olives are also grown.

Needless to say, everything in Givat Olam, the formal name of the farm, is done in strict accordance with *halacha* and under rabbinic supervision.

Chickens fed with organic food lay eggs with thicker shells, hence there is virtually no breakage. As a result Givat Olam does not produce powdered eggs. According to a company representative, the chickens are not injected with vaccinations posing the possibility of puncturing organs, but rather they receive vaccinations through an air spray.

What happens to a chicken when it can no longer lay eggs? In non-organic production the life of a chicken is extended through modern methods by several years, but at Givat Olam chickens are allowed to lay eggs for only eighteen months, the natural period in a chicken's life. Then, students learning *shechita* are brought in to practice their skills. Avri and his company tried to donate the kosher slaughter to charity organizations, but there was no interest. Experiments showed that it took some six hours to cook the chickens, and even then the meat was not tender enough to enjoy. The chickens are simply buried.

Passover posses special problems. Feeding stops two weeks before the holiday. For a day and a half the chickens are given no food! They are left to eat bits of food remaining in the coop (cleaning for Passover), then they are fed a special Passover diet (*chametz* no, *kitniyot* yes). In the past the organic food was purchased from an outside commercial source, but now production has been initiated in Itamar.

Goats are milked on a regular schedule, and there is no question about *chalav yisrael.* The rabbinic supervision is by unscheduled and unannounced visits, since all 50 workers at Givot Olam are Sabbath observant. Milk produced on Shabbos is done according to *halacha*, but it is processed in a separate line and not marketed as *mehadrin.*

Givot Olam sells more than thirty goat milk products. In addition to milk there is yoghurt (plain and flavored), spreading cheese, and sliced cheeses (requiring two or three months—but not longer—to produce). Want to taste? The restaurant is a nice beginning.

Monument to Joshua bin Nun and Synagogue

There are several other attractions in Itamar. Several meters outside the restaurant there is a curious monument to Joshua bin Nun and his conquest of the Land of Israel. The nearby synagogue (the first permanent building to be erected in this part of Itamar) is of unusual architecture. A local tradition also requires that there always be someone learning in the synagogue, even as part of his paid agricultural "work" schedule.

Ancient Winery

Itamar also hosts the largest ancient winery in the Shomron. Parts of the wine press have been uncovered, as well as an extremely large underground storage cavern. Even the shelves that once held jars of wine can be seen today.

Entrance to the cave has been facilitated by an enlarged opening, better steps, and electricity. First steps have been taken to convert part of the cave into a museum detailing the ancient tradition of making wine.

Visits to Itamar are best made by prior arrangement. The local council can be reached at 02-997-5667.

Note. No mention of Itamar can be complete without mentioning the cold-blooded murder of Udi and Ruth Fogel and three of their children on March 12, 2011. This was a tragic incident, but it should absolutely not deter tourists from visiting Itamar.

P'sagot

P'sagot is a Jerusalem bedroom-community founded in the early 1980s just east of Ramallah/Al-Birah. The settlement, now numbering more than 2,300 residents, was once accessible through Al-Birah, where many of the people would shop. Those days reflect a bygone era, and economics have changed. Today one picks up a bypass road in P'isgat Zeev.

Although P'sagot is primarily residential, there is one noteworthy attraction that makes a visit worthwhile for tourists.

According to local tradition, as P'sagot began to develop, Meir Berg started to plant orchards and vineyards, only to find a wine press and an olive oil press possibly dating to the period of the Second Temple. (He reportedly also discovered remnants of a biblical settlement in the area, which he took to be Ha-Ai mentioned in the Book of Joshua. Some archeologists, however, contend that the more accurate location is in the nearby Arab village of De'ir Dibwan, excavated in 1954. (See Beit El entry)

For the modern winery see Kosher Wine Guide.

Ofra

Ofra, taking its name from the nearby Biblical Ophrah (Joshua 18:23), is another settlement in the Shomron area. Some of the land is on an abandoned Jordanian army base. Now numbering three thousand residents, Ofra was authorized in February 1974 by the Labor government then in power. Here, too, there is a large wine industry. See Kosher Wine Guide.

Shilo

Tel Shilo

For over three hundred years Shilo was the resting place of the Mishkan and the focal point of Jewish worship and triennial pilgrimage. The ancient area known as Tel Shilo covers about 30.5 dunhams, and is now a popular tourist site. During recent centuries the entire area was not populated. A nearby modern settlement, now home to more than 2,300 residents, was established in 1978. Although there had been initial excavations by a Danish group in 1926–1932, archeological digging at Tel Shilo using modern methods was first undertaken in the early 1980s.

For religious tourists a visit to Tel Shilo is a step back into history. The site is impressive as one looks out at a commanding view of the adjacent valley and Path of the Patriarchs, the ancient road connecting Beersheva to the south and Shechem (Nablus) to the north. (For security reasons one cannot traverse most of this road, however a section in Gush Etzion is under Israeli control.)

Portions of walls judged to belong to the Canaanite city have been unearthed, and with them there is a practical *halachic* issue. Does this mean that the Scroll of Esther should be read on the fourteenth or fifteenth day of Adar?

Remains of ancient Shilio

Archeological evidence suggests that the pre-Israelite city was conquered without a destructive battle. The lower portion of the uncovered wall, thought to be Canaanite, is made of uneven stones; a higher portion, judged to be of a later date, had more regular construction. One must remember that dating is little more than an educated guess by archeologists, and very often conclusions are a matter of controversy.

There is also a significant question about a city surrounded by a wall in the time of Joshua (hence Purim on Adar 15 as in Jerusalem). It is unclear if the thought-to-be Canaanite city was completely encircled by walls in all four directions, or if the height and slope of the mountain provided desired protection. In any event, the entrances to the biblical city from three directions have been rediscovered.

For the record there has been a rabbinic decision regarding Purim. Residents of Shilo keep two days of Purim—the first to satisfy *halachic* requirements and the second because the city's status is not absolutely clear (to avoid doubt as is done in numerous other Israeli cities).

The evidence proving the authenticity of Tel Shilo as the correct site is quite convincing, although the exact location of where the Mishkan was located is not at all clear. The earliest description of the site is Judges 21:13. The identification is reinforced by remnants of a synagogue from the period very late Second Temple or the Talmud. (The synagogue was reportedly more or less intact as late as 1335.)

Shilo area where Mishkan possibly was (Sheina)

A room with numerous large storage vessels (now being evaluated by archeologists) was uncovered. Were these containers used to keep food for the thousands of pilgrims who would come to Shilo in the time of the Mishkan? Were they somehow related to the worship? Were they used by Shilo residents after worship moved to Jerusalem? Even if the answer is never really found, it makes one think of the practical *realia* of Biblical times.

Another significant finding is a lamp typical of the Second Temple period. The lamp carries the letter "*shin*." And, archeologists have unearthed dozens of ancient coins.

Not everything is understood. The use of nearby springs is obvious, but the use of a series of interconnected tunnels is a mystery.

As is typical with many archeological sites in Israel, there are numerous layers, and the material of Jewish interest tends to be in the lowest sections. From top to bottom Tel Shilo has medieval construction, Byzantine churches, and Biblical remnants ending roughly in the Bar Kochba era. The churches are a strong indication of the importance that Christians attached to the site. It is also curious that after the Moslem conquest mosaic images of animals (forbidden according to most interpretations of *Shari'a*—Moslem law) were destroyed, yet at least one ceramic cross was left intact. Current plans are to dig on lower levels to unearth more material of Jewish interest.

A visit to the antiquities at Shilo is certainly recommended. It is an opportunity to refresh our memory about a period in Jewish history and to pray. For those who offer their supplications, may they be answered like Chana in Shilo!

For reservations (Adults NIS12, Children NIS10) and guided tours in Hebrew or English (NIS250) call 02-994-4019. The site is open 0800–1600 Sunday-Thursday and 0800–1300 Friday, and a usual visit takes about ninety minutes. A cellular telephone guide is also available. Shomer Shabbat. A kosher restaurant with rabbinic supervision is adjacent to the site.

Olives & Olive Oil *(See color plate 19, p 106)*

Meshek Achiya is a prize-winning olive oil company located in the industrial zone of Shilo since 2004. Its leading house blend is a combination of *souri, picual* and *arbequina* varieties. In addition to olive oil, Meshek Achiya also markets *souri* and *manzanillo* packaged olives. Sales are possible on site.

The owners are Sabbath observant. Products are under the kashrut supervision of Chug Chatam Sofer-Petach Tikva, Rabbanut Matei Binyamin (*mehadrin*), and the O-K.

The best season to visit is from Succot through Chanukah, but tourists are always welcome to tour the factory. A short tour comes with an introduction to the production of olive oil. Open Sunday–Thursday 0800–1500. To arrange a visit call 02-940-1313. Access by public transportation is impractical.

Winery – See Kosher Wine Guide

Across the River

General Information

Jordan in General

A visit to Jordan can be a rewarding experience for the tourist, but careful and prudent behavior is a basic guideline. There is a definite trend toward the Islamization of Jordan. Traditional dress is more common than ten years ago, and there are more mosques than ever before. Anti-Semitic acts, however, are strictly outlawed, and the government has clamped down on openly inciting conduct.

After dozens of trips I can say that I have never encountered any unpleasant problems. Low profile behavior, though, is always recommended.

Crossing into Jordan

Jerusalem can be an appropriate starting point for a quick trip to Jordan. Many people make the mistake of basing themselves in Eilat, then going to Petra for a day. They spend a disproportionate percentage of their time on the bus and miss the many attractions in central and northern Jordan.

Travel to and from Jordan can be done from the Beit Shean, Eilat and Allenby crossings. A Jordanian visa is available upon arrival at the first two crossings; a visa must be obtained in advance from the consular section of a Jordanian Embassy before crossing the Allenby Bridge, where only foreign (non-Israeli) passports are allowed. Israel exit tax can be paid by credit card at all three locations, but it is double at the Allenby Bridge. If you are traveling from Jerusalem, the Allenby Bridge is to be preferred despite the increased fee. (The bridge is sometimes closed due to large volumes of travelers, partularly on Fridays in the summer.)

To reach Amman from Jerusalem, the most practical route is to take a taxi (shared or private) from the Damascus Gate to the Allenby Bridge. There is bus service roughly once an hour across the bridge to Jordan. Alternatively, there is a private "VIP" service that is quite costly and dispatches cars upon request. Once across the Allenby Bridge the easiest method to reach Amman is by taxi; there is a very inexpensive local bus, but the trip is not at all comfortable, and the schedule is erratic. Return travel from

Jordan to Israel is by similar method with a Jordanian exit tax charged at the border. Use of the other crossings is best either for experienced travelers or for groups, since there is no convenient regular bus service.

Licenses

All Jordanian tour guides are licensed by the Ministry of Tourism & Antiquities. They also all speak English. It is illegal for someone without such a government license to accept payment for giving tours.

Eating Kosher

The best bet is to shop for groceries in one of the branches of C-Town, an American chain with some imported products carrying United States kashrut organization symbols. Safeway has fewer foreign products with kashrut symbols. Fresh fruits and vegetables for salads are plentiful in Jordan. This may be supplemented by a few cans of food (sardines, tuna, etc.) that you can bring along.

Jordan is hot in the summer, but cans of cold drinks and bottles of mineral water are sold in many places.

Note: It is not proper to eat or drink in public during the daylight hours of Ramadan (the month when Moslems fast from early morning to sunset).

In short, food should not be an overwhelming concern, particularly for the typical visit of only a few days. (There are no synagogues in Jordan. A Shabbat visit is not recommended.)

Amman

It is clear from archaeological findings in Ain Ghazal (eastern Amman) that the area was settled in a very early period. In the thirteenth century BCE Amman was called Rabbath Ammon based upon the Ammonites who are mentioned in the Torah. Over the centuries Amman was conquered by the Assyrians, the Persians, the Macedonians, the Nabateans, and the Romans. Ptolemy II Philadelphus named the city Philadelphia, which later was renamed Amman in the third century CE. The city was out of the way and remained insignificant until the building of the Hejaz Railroad. (For those interested there is a small museum adjacent to the central railroad station in Amman; there still are round trips to Syria using Ottoman-era cars, but travel is recommended only up to the international border.) In 1921 then-Emir Abdullah (later King Abdullah I; 1882-1951) made Amman his capital.

Citadel

The Museum in the Citadel, located atop a mountain with a strategic view of Amman, houses part of the Dead Sea Scrolls. There are also artifacts from the Biblical era of the Patriarchs. The display is poor and dated, but that should be changed when the new National Museum of Jordan finally opens after numerous delays and the exhibits are transferred. Optimistically, the new museum should be open by the time this book is published.

Martyrs' Memorial

In 1977 Jordanian King Hussein (1935-1999) ordered the establishment of a national memorial to soldiers who fell in the line of duty since the Arab Revolt of 1916–1919. Not long thereafter the Martyrs' Memorial, designed by Victor Adel Bisharat (1920–1996), opened in Amman with the goal of enshrining the memory of those who gave their lives for their country.

The museum has models recreating 1948 battles in Bab El-Wad/ Latrun. The Arab goal was to cut the communications and supply lines between besieged Jerusalem and Zionist forces in the Tel Aviv and Shefela areas. Another of the items in the memorial is a large painting (to the left of the entrance) depicting a fierce battle at Jerusalem's Flower (Herod's) Gate in 1948.

The years that followed saw repeated conflict with Israel. There were Israeli successes. There were Jordanian successes. Amongst the items on display in the museum are captured Israeli military rations and an IDF rifle.

Cities of the Plain

There is an impressive list of possible locations in Jordan for Biblical sites, for example in the time of Sodom and Amora when the Cities of the Plain might well have been on both sides of modern borders, but very little is certain, and in any case there is little other than Hor HaHar of true religious significance.

Dibon (Dhiban)

In 1868 the Reverend Frederick Augustus Klein(1827-1903)of the Church Missionary Society at Jerusalem made an historic find in what had been the Moabite capital centuries before. He came across what is now known as the Moabite Stone. There was no complex excavation. The heavy black basalt stone was lying on the ground! Unfortunately, the local inhabitants had broken part of the stone, however the French stepped in, purchased the fragments, and sent the restored stone to Paris for display in the Louvre.

The inscription on the stone is the record in Phoenician of the wars of Mesha, king of Moab, with Israel. The inscription mentions King Omri (9th century BCE), and relates the war with the Jews from the Moabite perspective.

There have been numerous excavations of more recent date in Dibon. City walls, a defense tower, various building foundations and pottery unearthed in some of the digging suggest settlement from the Early Bronze Age (*c.* 3200–*c.* 2300 BCE), but there are numerous gaps in subsequent chronology. In any event, there is nothing of any Jewish connection to be seen today in Dibon. Interest is more for the professional archeologist. In effect Dibon is just another village with a rich past unconnected with its current condition.

Grave of Aaron the Cohen

Hor HaHar, or Jebel Haroun in Arabic is the accepted grave of Aaron, who like Moses died before he could reach the Promised Land. The site, however, is not appropriate for all tourists. The grave is atop a mountain in the Petra enclave. Particularly on the *yahrzeit*, Rosh Chodesh Av, a few religious Jews sometimes make the four to six hour trek to the grave, often assisted by the hire of donkeys. At the top there is a thirteenth century Moslem monument marking the spot. Any Jewish flavor to the visit is only that spirit which is self-generated by the visitor.

Advance arrangements and hire of a donkey with guide are highly recommended.

Mount Nebo and Madaba

The Children of Israel wandered through Jordan before entering the Land of Israel, and Moses gazed out at the land before he died. We are told in the Torah that his grave is unknown. Thus, there is absolutely no reason to give credence to the tourist site hailing Moses' death on Mount Nebo, a location fixed in a "vision" in the fourth century by Helena, a noted non-Jew.

Ten kilometers from that mountain view there sits the town of Madaba, known for the famous sixth century mosaic map that so clearly depicts Jerusalem in the context of an area that stretches from Southern Syria to the Egyptian city of Thebes. Again, however, Jewish interest is limited by the location of the mosaic—on the floor of a local church. (A replica of a segment of the map is on display in Jerusalem's Cardo.)

Just off the road from Jerusalem to Jericho in the West Bank there is Nebi Musa. This is a Moslem site connected with their interpretation of Moses. It has absolutely no Jewish meaning.

On the Road South

As Roman troops advanced southward from victory at Masada to battle against the Nabateans in Petra, *en route* they attacked and slaughtered Jews who had fled Jerusalem. Near the small town of Zora there are first century CE Jewish graves, later incorporated into a Byzantine non-Jewish cemetery.

Qasr Al-Amir

The Roman era historian, Josephus, relates (Antiquities XII–XIV) a detailed narrative. For twenty-two years during the reigns of Ptolmey III Euergetes and Ptolmey IV Philopator, Joseph of Tobiades was a tax collector based in Jerusalem. In 209 BCE the aging Joseph sent his son with lavish gifts to Hyrcanus to celebrate the birth of Ptolmey V. The son became a favorite of Hyrcanus, whose brothers became jealous and attempted to kill him. He fled Jerusalem and took refuge in the Trans-Jordanian desert, where he built a well-guarded fortress.

The fortress is hard to reach by public transportation. Even by car it can be hard to find because of poor road signs. There is a small museum next to the fortress.

Kosher Wine Guide

Touring Wineries

Looking for something "different" to do in the Jerusalem area? A tour of standard and boutique wineries can be a fascinating option and a very different introduction to economic life. It can also be an excellent opportunity to stock up on an unusual wine for Purim, or a quality wine for Passover or the year round. Superior non-sweet wines are relatively new to Israel.The Judean Hills have known wineries since ancient times; the industry, however, has changed dramatically since the early 1990s. There are numerous key wineries to visit in the Greater Jerusalem area. Some wineries produce wines that are excellent. Others are just good. And, there are those that "need improvement." There are also wineries that face a dubious future due to problems of quality, distribution, and cash flow. Taste is subjective. Let each person judge for himself.

The various wineries are listed together for the reader's convenience. Wineries without rabbinic supervision are not listed.

Readers should be cautioned that many boutique wineries began operation without rabbinic supervision, then only later did they receive kashrut approval. For this reason each and every bottle should be checked for supervision.

Very often winemakers explain that their wines have "always been kosher," but supervision only began only at a certain date. The reason is often stated that while production is limited, supervision is too expensive. Although this might be true, the observant consumer is taking a major risk in buying wine without proper kashrut certification.

It should also be remembered that non-*mevushal* (cooked, i.e. almost boiled) wines (and most quality wines are non-*mevushal*) should be poured only by Sabbath-observant Jews.

A good way to taste a sampling of Israeli kosher wines is at one of the wine festivals held throughout the year. The largest is the Wine Fair held annually in late summer on the grounds of the Israel Museum in Jerusalem.

To the South

Alon Shevut

Shraga Rosenberg, once the manager of a retirement home, had a dream. In 1994 he looked out at his garden in Efrat, remembered the blessing of wine given to Yehudah (see Genesis 49:11 and Rashi), and decided to make blackberry wine in his basement. From fruit wines in a home-spun operation, his efforts have evolved into the Gush Etzion Winery, a modern facility on the road to Alon Shevut and Kfar Etzion. Yes, the company still makes blackberry wine, but now it is more famous for its top of the line Cabernet Franc, which won a gold medallion in November 2007 at the Terravino contest in Israel. All of their numerous wines are O-U for Passover. Want to taste? Attached to the winery there is a dairy restaurant, where wines can be bought either by the glass or by the bottle.

Additional information about the winery and restaurant can be obtained by calling 02-930-9220.

Bat Ayn

Today the tradition of local wine making continues based on ancient tradition—the Ferency Winery where production by Gershon Ferency and his family is from organically grown grapes.

Ferency, an orthodox Jew and former yeshiva student, is another winemaker who came to the trade entirely by chance. When Elazar ceased to be a *moshav*, the Jewish Agency took back the farm land that had been given to grow nut trees, and they issued a tender for new agricultural uses. Ferency and four partners submitted a winning bid to plant wine vineyards, but within a year only Ferency remained. The first planting was in 1993, and the first wine was made five years later, but by another producer. Sales of Ferency-made wine began for home use only during the *shemita* of 2008; in the following year equipment was purchased, production expanded, and in 2010 marketing started.

There is a big difference between growing grapes and making wine, so one of the steps that Ferency took was to enroll in a distance learning course at the University of California-Davis.

The house specialties are two white wines and two reds: Chardonnay, Sauvignon Blanc, Merlot, and Cabernet Sauvignon (all certified to be organic). Every winemaker has his own methods, and as Ferency explains, his winery also uses its own approach. Oak barrels are not used;

instead, an oak stave is placed into stainless steel containers to gain the value of oak tannin. A tip from the winemaker: To improve taste, after opening, pour the wine out of the bottle, then pour it back in, so that the wine can air out. The time of best taste is shortly after refilling the bottle, even if the wine is then refrigerated.

Supervision for *mehadrin* kashrut is by the Vaad Harabanut of Gush Etzion. There is no production during *shemita*. The winery bottling is limited; in 2008 the winery produced five thousand bottles and more the following year. The eventual goal is twelve thousand bottles per year.

Gershon Ferency is an extremely hospitable host and a personable individual (as well as a licensed tour guide). A tour of the winery can include the nearby ancient winery at the entrance to Bat Ayn.

Tours of the Ferency Winery (with tasting) can be arranged by calling 054-453-4425 or 02-993-2490.

Elazar

This small winery with a modest annual production of only four thousand bottles was founded in 2007 by Yohai Noy and Yaakov Goldberg. The winery makes Cabernet Sauvignon and Merlot. The grapes are grown in Gush Etzion. The Shalem blend (the pride of the vineyard) is aged eighteen months in French barrels; Jerusalem Mountains-Adom is aged fourteen months in French and American oak barrels. Sales are mostly at the winery. Kashrut supervision is by the Gush Etzion Rabbinate.

To arrange a tour and tasting call 02-993-2312 or 052-545-6759.

Kiryat Arba

Hebron Winery

The Hebron Winery was started in 1983. Their first wine and grape juice products were marketed for Passover 1984. About 90 percent of the production is sold outside Israel. That are sales in North America, but there are no exports to England. Or, as the owner, a Belzer *chassid* explains, "Not yet!" There is no formal tour of the winery, but during my visit I found the working staff full of fascinating information.

Hebron grapes are special. Although most grapes stay on the vine for six to eight weeks, several varieties of Hebron grapes remain on the vine for as much as five months. These grapes give the wine a special aroma. The Hebron winery products, however, are blends that include other grapes from elsewhere in Israel. The harvest season starts just after

Shavuot with grapes from the Jordan Valley and ends right before winter frost with Hebron varieties.

All Winery products are Kosher for Passover. During *shemita* the grapes come from lands owned by Arabs. Although the official rabbinic supervision is Belz, there is Beit Yosef certification that the products meet requirements for Sephardim.

Arabs use the Hebron grapes to make a special jam, but this has yet to enter the Jewish sector and kosher production.

Hevron Heights Winery

Although many people mistakenly think that this is a small winery that is producing wine only for export, reality is different. Yes, it is small, but only in physical space. For that reason there are no public tours. Even so, production is seven hundred thousand bottles per year.

It is hard to change initial impressions. At first it was thought to produce wine for export, but problems were encountered, particularly in France, because the company was over the Green Line. Today there are wines sent abroad (90 percent of the highest quality wine), but most of the production is for Israeli consumption. Perhaps part of the misconception is that many people do not see Hevron Heights wines, since they are sold only in wine stores and not in supermarkets or discount outlets.

Pinchas Murciano, an immigrant from France, started this business with the harvest of 2001, using grapes from non-Jewish sources because of the *shemita* year. His father had been in the wine business during the 1950s and 1960s in Fes, until Arab reaction to the Six Day War persuaded him that it would be best to emigrate. When Pinchas Murciano came to Israel, he worked in advertising for an international company that also was represented in the Arab world. With the outbreak of the Second Intifada, the company's business in Israel was downsized, and Murciano turned to the family tradition of wine. He decided to produce mostly quality wines, since he realized that the market was changing.

The Hevron Heights wines were kosher from startup. Let there be no question about the kashrut of these wines. Today they have no fewer than five rabbinic certificates (including O-U and Manchester) for marketing to non-Israelis.

As in many other wineries, French oak barrels are preferred over American. As Murciano explains, French oak gives a slower and more consistent taste. As to the grapes, 90 percent come from within fifty kilometers of Hevron.

Hevron Heights has three levels of quality. Noach is the most basic, not aged in oak barrels, sealed with a pressed-cork screw, and always *mevushal.* Yikvei Jerusalem is of intermediate quality, sealed with corks combining a synthetic inner layer with a natural outer layer, and again always *mevushal.* Jerusalem Heights is the highest quality, sealed with natural cork, placed in bottles from abroad, never *mevushal,* and according to Murciano hard to find since the small quantities in which it is produced are in high demand.

(For the record, the cork does influence the taste of wine, hence better wines are aged both in oak barrels and in the bottle, usually placed on its side for exposure to the cork.)

Murciano has plans for the future. He intends to move to a larger facility in Kiryat Arba and open a visitors' center where tourists can view the wine-making process, sample wines, and make purchases.

Tekoa

There is a small winery in Tekoa, which has produced Cabernet Sauvignon, some blended with Berlinka, a South African varietal. The owner of the winery, Dov Levy Neumand, immigrated to Israel from Lyons, France. Rabbinic supervision is by the Gush Etzion Rabbinate, and the wines are also certified organic by a professional organization.

Inside a small boutique winery

Neumand started in the wine business totally by happenstance. Initially he grew grapes for marketing by a large food conglomerate; however, he found the business not at all profitable. At his wife's suggestion, he started making wine first for the family, then for friends. In 1985 he entered the commercial market by selling five thousand bottles.

Now the winery is at a critical point of decision. After more than twenty-five years the vines are getting old and need to be replaced. Nor is Neumand the young man that he was thirty years ago when he first planted. He is hoping that a family member will take over. The marketing program has also been sized down with most sales at the winery (the basement of Neumand's home). The future of the winery is in limbo.

The winery can be reached by calling 02-996-4903. Advance notice is required for a visit (with tasting). Tours in Hebrew and French. There is no fee.

To the East

Mishor Adumim

Zion (Shorr) Winery

In 1848 Yitzchak Galin, the son of a chassidic Jew who had immigrated to Tsfat thirteen years earlier, started a very modest wine business on Rechov Hebron (today Rechov Ma'aleh Chaldieh) in Jerusalem's Old City. Jews always needed sacramental wine, so commercial production seemed to be a promising venture. Rather than contending with Ottoman bureaucracy, he used a business name of an extended family member—Shorr. Unbeknownst to this Karliner *chassid*, this upstart winery in rented space would burgeon a century and a half later into a strong series of companies producing wine and other alcoholic beverages.

People did not use street numbers. The store was "next to the public baths." It then expanded, adding a storage facility a couple of hundred meters away. As the winery family fondly relates, barrels of wine were stored next to one of the walls (an extension of the Western Wall), so that no one would mistakenly touch the area.

Ronald Storrs, the Mandate governor of Jerusalem, had his private and very definite ideas of how Jerusalem should develop, and in 1925 a ban on all "industry" in the Old City took effect. The area was for residence and small retail stores only. The winery had to move out.

As happenstance would be, the owner of the Shorr winery had just purchased a plot of land with a water source in the Beis Yisrael neighborhood (adjacent to Mea Shearim) for a residence and small store. Don't fight with reality! Plans quickly changed. The owner moved elsewhere, and a winery was built. The underground water source was used for cooling and for the manufacture of non-wine alcoholic beverages.

In many respects the move was fortuitous. After the anti-Jewish riots of 1929 and 1936 there was no longer a Jewish presence on Rechov Hebron. The Jews fled for their lives, some to the Jewish Quarter, but most to the New City outside the walls.

In the late 1920s Shorr wines (there was virtually no grape juice) became international. A large order for wine was received from Poland, but there was a condition. The Polish Jews wanted assurance that the Shorr wines were kosher. In those days before formal *hashgacha*, the owners of the company went to the religious court of the time and secured a letter attesting that they are *ehrliche yidden yir'ei shamayim* (G-d-fearing Jews).

As business expanded, the company became too large, and in 1944 it split. One brother kept the wine business, and another brother dealt with vodka, arak, and other spirits. A wall was built to divide the two businesses, and a door with the name Dr. Albert Abouchedid was erected at the new entrance. That door still stands today. Who was this doctor? No one knows. The door was bought second hand from a scrap-metal company!

The winery kept the name Shorr, and the hard-drinks operation took the name Arza after it eventually moved out (and went into the wine business as well). When the British came up with a new law—businesses could no longer have family names—they adopted the brand, "Zion."

Elisha Shorr joined his father as an accountant in the re-organized winery in 1944 while he was also learning in Etz Chaim Yeshiva, but times were difficult. In August 1948 this Karliner *chassid* was fighting in the Palmach. On a day off and just outside the winery he walked a few steps behind his brother, a nephew, and another family member. A Jordanian artillery shell killed the three, but he was saved virtually unscathed. Elisha spent two years in the army, then started to work full time.

As Elisha relates, one of the famous Shorr customers was Dr. Moritz Moshe Wallach (1866–1957), head of Shaare Zedek Hospital and in earlier years an enthusiastic student of HaRav Yosef Chaim Sonnenfeld (1848–1932). He trusted no one for the kashrut of wine (except for the Shorr family, of course), not even his Sabbath observant driver. In the days before bottled wine, Wallach would arrive at the winery and personally supervise the transfer of wine from big barrels into tubes, and then into containers which he brought.

Even under Israeli rule times were difficult in Beit Yisrael. New zoning laws in the early 1950s meant fines and legal battles for the winery. Water was scarce (sold by ration tickets at one point), and as a result running the business was a challenge. But, there was nowhere to go until well after the Six Day War, when the winery was finally offered a six dunham plot of land in the Mishor Adumim Industrial Zone. The company moved gradually between 1982 and 1986.

There are no compromises with kashrut. Supervision is by the Eida. Absolutely no water is added to either the wine or grape juice, nor is there grape concentrate. *Orla* is not a question, since it takes at least five years from the time of planting to grow a good grape for wine. All wines marketed in Israel that are *mevushal* (cooked) are clearly labeled as such. And, all company employees without exception are Sabbath observant.

What is in the old Beit Yisrael winery? The water source has been dried up. There is a storage area for sales to customers who want to buy directly, fearing that grocers might tamper with the kashrut of the wine. And much of the winery has been renovated into a synagogue and *kolel.*

Times have changed. Grape juice, which once constituted about 5 percent of production, is now in much stronger demand. On the other hand, since the advent of synthetic vinegar (kosher for Passover), there are only minimal requests for wine vinegar. Many Israeli wines are in bottles labeled שדה קובקב (new bottle), a throwback to the days of reusable bottles. Today all Zion bottles are new (usually made abroad and needing immersion in a *mikva*, if the consumer reuses them).

In 2000 the company also decided to address the new wine market of ultra-orthodox Jews. In addition to sweet wines, Zion now produces such varieties as Merlot and Cabernet Sauvignon.

When asked about the quality of wine, Yossi Shorr (in charge of marketing) explains that grapes are brought specially from various parts of Israel (Spain during the last *shemita,* and Cyprus before that). Taking pride in his company's product, he offered that knowledge is a significant part of making wine, "It is impossible to make a good wine from bad grapes, but it is quite possible to make a bad wine from good grapes." Shor uses extensive controls to insure a superior product.

A couple of consumer tips. The wines of 2006 are particularly of better quality. The quality controls on grape juice are much less exacting, and taste can vary even with the same marketing label.

Visits to the winery are welcomed but must be arranged in advance. Telephone: 02-535-2540.

HaCormim Winery

At work in the winery

As described, Zion (Shorr) Wines split in 1944 into Zion and Arza. The latter was managed by four partners, a rather unwieldy arrangement, so in 1958 the four decided to split and established yet another winery in the larger Shorr Family — the HaCormim Winery on Rechov Nagiara in Jerusalem's Givat Shaul neighborhood. (In the early 1980s they moved to their current location in Mishor Adumim.) The new company started under Eida supervision, but in the 1970s they changed to Aguda.

In those days Israeli wines were quite unsophisticated. As Yechiel Shorr, the company's managing director explains, the market was almost exclusively sweet wine for kiddush. According to Shorr, "For every twenty bottles of sweet wine, perhaps one bottle of dry wine was sold." People would even call the dry wine by the derogatory epithet, "sour wine." The market, however, began to change in the early 1960s with the arrival of immigrants from Hungary and Roumania. Suddenly dry wine became much more in demand, but the varieties available were not at all sophisticated.

Grape juice is by no means a traditional favorite. It gained mass popularity only in the late 1960s and early 1970s. Today grape juice comprises the clear majority of HaCormim's sales.

Immigration has a decided effect on the market, as newcomers bring their tastes and desires. This is not true only with wine. Even in its early years HaCormim did not limit its production to wine. In the company's initial days their arak outsold vodka virtually 99:1, reflecting Moroccan tastes. Since the large Russian immigration of the 1990s that ratio has been totally reversed. Liqueur preferences have moved in the direction of imports from abroad, and sales of Israeli products have decreased so significantly that HaCormim has closed that line of production.

Yechiel Shorr has made a conscious decision about the business direction of HaCormim. He does not intend to enter the market of elegant wines. He prefers to concentrate on making a quality wine for the mass market. As he explains, "Boutique wines started about fifteen years ago at most, and most companies do not last." Speaking quite frankly he added, "Ninety percent of the buyers do not know what they are drinking … they buy boutique wines as a status symbol."

In the same spirit Shorr ventured that many drinks enjoy a short period of popularity, then demand decreases drastically. He offered the example of sangría (a typically Iberian mixture of inexpensive wine, fruit juice, a sweetener such as honey or sugar, and spices). This was popular in kosher circles in the 1970s, then the fad ended.

Wine vinegar is another product that was never in demand, hence HaCormim does not market the little that they do produce. In fact, today no *mehadrin* Israeli company markets wine vinegar.

What kind of wine does HaCormim sell? One could almost say, "The sweeter, the better." High on the list is Conditon, a favorite of those who like a sweet taste.

HaCormim wines usually carry the company label, but their grape juice can be hard to find by the uninitiated. They cater to the mass market, and in Israel a big private label customer for grape juice is Supersol. In the UK the same philosophy has prompted them to sell their product through the HaMutag label.

If you are looking for a Merlot, Chardonnay, or other sophisticated wine, HaCormim is not in the business. If, however, you want a traditional kiddush wine or grape juice, HaCormim is a possibility.

To the West

Beit Meir

HaMasrek is one of fashionable "boutique wineries" that have sprung up across Israel. While large operations such as Carmel specialize in mass production and popular prices, this smaller winery is another of the family operations that concentrate on gourmet products for the wine connoisseur. HaMasrek is run by the Greengrass family.

Avraham Greengrass was a Jerusalem tailor, but during the Arab siege of Jerusalem, he had trouble making ends meet. His ration book did not allow purchase of enough food to feed his family. So, when Beit Meir was established in 1950 on the ruins of an abandoned Arab village some ten miles west of Jerusalem, Greengrass uprooted his family and moved into the new settlement. He left needle and thread behind, and became a farmer, planting a small field and raising chickens. Food was no longer a problem.

Beit Meir, named after Meir Bar-Ilan (1880-1949) and restricted to Sabbath observant residents, was a quiet place to live. To the south is what has become the Israel Path for hiking, and to the north is the Burma Road, the makeshift road built during the War of Independence to bring supplies to Jerusalem.

Times changed. Israeli economics of the 1980s and 1990s were not the same as the 1950s and 1960s. It was no longer feasible to depend on a small farm and chicken eggs. It was then that Nahum Greengrass, Avraham's grandson, decided to convert the chicken coup into a winery. In 2000 HaMasrek wines went into production.

When Palmach fighters were constructing the Burma Road, they looked at the trees in the area and described them as bristles on "a brush" (Hebrew, *"masrek"*). The name stuck. There is the Masrek Nature Reserve next to Beit Meir, and Greengrass decided to call his wine company by the same word.

Grape vines reach their best flavor twelve years after planting, and proper wines require two or three years to prepare. Rather than quickly producing an inferior product, Greengrass contracted with nearby Shoresh to purchase quality grapes from mature vines. HaMasrek, however, never bought all of the grapes grown in Shoresh; the contract stipulates that the winery does not buy *heter mechira* products of the *shemita* year.

HaMasrek produces some twenty-five thousand bottles of wine each year. Cabernet Sauvignon, Chardonnay and Gewürztraminer are the house standards, but as good as the wines are, the question of marketability arose. How does one enter foreign markets, where most wine is sold?

Kashrut was not a question for HaMasrek. The wines are not *mevushal* (cooked/boiled), and clearly labeled as such. In addition to local Israeli supervision, HaMasrek came under O-U supervision as well. (Each supervision sends its own inspectors to the winery.) Workers are members of the Greengrass family, who are all Sabbath-observant.

Nachum Greengrass traveled several times to the United States, looking to find a niche in the American market. Advice was plentiful. "Try not to compete," was the common line. "It will be hard to sell another Chardonnay or another Gewürztraminer. There already are numerous brands on the market." So, Greengrass pondered the issue and came up with an innovative solution—a totally new product—King's Blend, a delicate combination of three wines in different proportions and blended together by a house-developed process. Sales began, and success was at hand. Although most sales are in North America, the HaMasrek wines are available in England as well (primarily in the Greater London area).

Traveling to Japan or China? Do not be surprised to see HaMasrek wines in the major cities. Lately, that has been a very good sales point.

If you are in the Beit Meir area, a visit to the winery is certainly a positive experience. Hours are Fridays 1000–1500 (closes earlier in the winter) and during the week by prior arrangement. Tel. 02-570-1759 or 054-483-0827. The winery is closed to visitors during August and September, when grapes are received and processed. The closing is by instruction of kashrut supervisors and by the Ministry of Health. During the one-hour tour, explanations of the wines are given in Hebrew and English by Nahum Greengrass, so answers to questions are authoritative. There is no fee, and the visit includes wine tasting. Wheelchair accessible.

Transportation by Egged Bus 186 from Jerusalem or by car, exiting the Jerusalem–Tel Aviv Highway at Hemed Junction.

Beit Zayit

Not all businesses are a success. Some wineries start out as a hobby. Others have problems as the founders become older. In all probability there will be smaller wineries bought out by competition. And there are those that fail after cost analysis.

The Zmora Winery once in Beit Zayit is now closed. In its day it became kosher in 2004 (O-K) and produced Cabernet Sauvignon, Merlot, Cabernet Franc, Chardonnay, and Viognier. Their bottles are now oenology collectors' items.

Emek Ha'ela

Agur

This is a small but growing winery established in 1997 and kosher since the vintage of 2007. Shuki Yashuv is the chief wine maker and expert; he works with a Spanish partner. Primary products are Cabernet Sauvignon, Merlot, Petit Verdot, and Cabernet Franc. Visits, usually between 1000 and 1600 on Sunday through Thursday and with shorter hours on Friday, must be coordinated in advance with the Agur Visitors Center, at 054-459-9672.

Givat Yesaiahu – Kela David

In 1992 this was the first boutique winery established in the Judean Hills, based on wine production knowledge brought from Italy. Only weekend visits arranged in advance are possible, since this is not a full-time business. Production is small but the Kela David label now includes both white (Italian-style dry and semi-dry) and red (Petit Sira, Merlot, Cabernet) wines, which are available only at the winery and not in stores. Current production is under rabbinical supervision. The winery also produces olive oil.

Telephone: 052-222-9945. Business No. 61, Givat Yeshaiahu.

Neve Michael – Yaffo Winery

The business began in the 1998s in Tel Aviv-Yafo, hence the name. It had stated out as the hobby of a physiotherapist, who had spent time in Strassbourg, where he met his wife, and was introduced to wine culture. Soon the company (really a Celniker Family business) moved to Tel Aviv, then finally to its current location. The company has been kosher (O-K, Beit Yosef, local rabbinate) since 2009. (The earlier non-kosher bottles are not on sale.) The winemakers pride themselves on French methodology. In charge is the owner's son, Stephane Celniker, who learned wine-making in France. A Chardonnay blend (85 percent Chardonnay, 15 percent Sauvignon Blanc aged three months in oak barrels) is one of the first kosher wines that the company has produced. Another is Merlot Syrah (one year 70 percent Merlot, 30 percent Syrah aged twelve months in French and American barrels, but changing percentages according to the vintage).

A sales point is still maintained at Rozov 15, Tel Aviv. Telephone: 03-647-4834. Visits to the winery are on Fridays by appointment. Since tours and tasting are in good part outdoors, visits during inclement weather are not recommended. The fee is NIS35 with unlimited tasting; the fee is waived if purchases are made.

To contact the winery call 054-452-3201.

Eshtaol

Flam Winery

This is a family operation in every sensed. Golan and Gilad Flam started the winery in 1998. Golan learned the art of wine making in Italy; Gilad is a lawyer by training, and contributed his knowledge of business administration to the enterprise. Their father, Israel Flam, a thirty-five year veteran of Carmel-Mizrahi, is the wine maker with knowledge of the trade from South Africa and from the University of California-Davis.

After years of operation without kashrut supervision a strategic decision was made to a major extent in view of the export market. Beginning with the vintage of 2010 (introduced to the market in 2012–2014 depending on the wine), the winery became formally kosher (O-K, Beit Yosef, and the local rabbinate).

The Flam winery is middle-sized, annually producing over one hundred thousand bottles. The house specialty is dry wine, which is available in several varieties.

All visits and events must be arranged in advance. For further details and bookings call Ms. Liatte Nicole Miller at 054-211-3324 or 02-992-9923.

A tour including wine tasting (usually fifty to eighty minutes) costs NIS60 per person .The wine tour with the addition of a rich platter of artisanal breads and cheese is NIS100 per person. All food is also under local rabbinical supervision.

Ruth Winery *(See color plate 20, p 106)*

If you are looking for a very different wine experience, the Ruth Winery near Shilat Junction is an excellent choice. The parents of Tal Miara were amongst the founders of this small settlement near Modi'in. As the years went by Tal went to law school and earned a degree. He started to practice law, but in 2001 he added another profession to his skills. He had become proficient in making European wines, so he decided to try his hand at the trade. From an original three barrels his family enterprise now produces twenty thousand bottles per year. There is gratis tasting every Friday from 10 a.m. until 2 p.m., with sales of bottles that catch your fancy. In the summer and in pre-holidays seasons there are wine events — wine, boutique cheese, olives, bread, and plenty of live music in a rustic and very friendly outdoor setting on Thursday evenings, usually about once a month. It is a memorable event, a fine way to spend an evening, and the NIS 40 entrance fee is truly modest. For schedule and driving instructions, Telephone: 054-677 8900 (mobile).

Mata

Nevo wines were started in 2002 by Nevo Chazan on Moshav Mata. What started as a hobby became a small family business. Production is about five thousand bottles per year—an operation totally run by the Chazan family with sales only on premises. The wines are kosher under the supervision of HaRav Charlop beginning with the 2010 vintage. The kosher wines in the new vintage are Merlot, Cabernet Sauvignon, and Petit Verdot (including some blended combinations).

Visits and small parties can be arranged by calling 052-607-1780. Closed on the Sabbath. Moshav Mata is close to Beitar Illit on Route 375 descending to Beit Shemesh.

Mesilat Tziyon – Katz Winery
(See color plate 21, p 107)

Yaacov Katz, a child of Holocaust survivors, established his winery in 2000, and it became kosher with the vintages of 2008 (local rabbinical supervision) and 2009 (O-K). He also restricted the refreshments he serves to dairy only, and that also came under rabbinical supervision. Why? When asked if he has recovered the investment of being kosher, he replied that he hopes this will encourage business, but that is not the reason for his decision.

Katz tells an interesting story. For many years he worked as a physiologist and bio-chemist, then when he went on pension, he started his winery. He was always an avid reader, and scientific issues interest him. For example, he grows all of his grapes organically. He is also a very informed source about the alcohol in wine, sugar, and diabetes (though he refrains from giving "medical" advice for legal reasons).

At one stage he read an interesting research report that alarmed him—the best way to delay Alzheimer's disease or postpone its onset is to take a retirement job that involves mental activity and puts the brain to work. What should he do? He enjoyed making wine, but for the most part it is not exactly an intellectual challenge.

One day he was talking with a religious relative and describing his quandary. The relative, a rabbi working in Ponevez Yeshiva in Bnei Braq, had a suggestion. If Katz wants to challenge his mind and stay mentally fresh, learn Gemara! Katz accepted the advice. So, for two years he joined a specially-designed learning program for "older" students. He certainly exercised his mental capabilities, but something else happened as well. He developed a new understanding of Judaism and decided that he had to change his life style. One of the first steps was to make the winery kosher and cease Sabbath operations. On a visit to the winery one sees the *mashgiach* and a *chareidi* assistant busy taking instructions and making wine.

House specialties are off-dry and port wines, but there is also a semi-dry and a dry red reserve. And there is a 12.5 percent "lite" wine. Some companies dilute their "lite" wine with water, but Katz has another system. He dilutes his wine with grape juice, so there are no *halachic* problems.

As a general rule the primary difference between dry and sweet wines is the level of residual sugar remaining after fermentation, though there are other factors. In simplistic terms off-dry wine is medium on the scale, not sweet and not dry. There are very few if any kosher wines labeled "off-dry" that are produced in Israel.

One of the major attractions of the winery is just a conversation with Yaacov Katz. He is a fascinating person.

Visits to the winery must be arranged in advance, and they can be in Hebrew, English and German. Tours of the winery can include just tasting or a dairy brunch. This is one of the few wineries that also offer a course in the art of wine tasting!

To arrange a visit to the winery call 050-257-3950. Turn south on Route 38 from the Jerusalem–Tel Aviv Highway, then turn right at the sign to Mesilat Tziyon. After a very short distance turn right again down a poorly-paved road, and follow the signs to the winery.

Nes Harim – Katlav Winery

Every winery has its own story, and this one is no different. In 1998 Yosi Yittach left his profession as an architect to seek a quiet life with his family. He went into wine making, first learning the trade from a Persian friend of the family who brought knowledge from "the old country," where there was a strong oenophile tradition. He then supplemented his education with courses. First production was in 2004, and by 2006 he was bottling better quality wines certainly worth sampling. House specialties are Cabernet Sauvignon, Merlot, and Chardonnay (10 percent Viognier), but what is unique is Wadi Katlav, a house blend (50 percent Cabernet Sauvignon, 30 percent Merlot, 20 percent Petit Verdot)—different from an older version that had 50 percent Sauvignon, 40 percent Merlot and 10 percent Syrah—aged in French oak barrels for eighteen months before bottling.

Yittach is Sabbath observant, and the winery is under the supervision of both the local Rabbinate and the O-K. There has been no *shemita* production. For reasons of kashrut visitors are not allowed into the barrel room, but it can be seen through a glass window. Yittach stresses, however, that visitors are welcome (preferably but not exclusively on Friday mornings) by prior arrangement. Unlike many wineries, wine tasting is under rabbinic kashrut supervision.

Katlav is not only a winery! It is a place with a very friendly atmosphere in which one can host a "culinary event" or party for groups ranging from twenty-five to fifty persons. The menu, under rabbinical supervision, is extremely tempting, and needless to say it is accompanied by wines with the house label.

Telephone: 02-570-1404. Signs lead from the entrance to Nes Harim right to the winery.

If you are interested in learning more about wines from the Judean Hills, Yosi Yittach is the head of the Judean Hills Winery Association.

Ramat Raziel *(See color plate 22, p 107)*

It is an unlikely story. Eli Ben Zaken, the owner of Domaine du Castel Wines, was born in Alexandria, Egypt. His father worked for an Italian company, and in 1958 when political repression became intolerable, the family emigrated to Milano. Eli was then sent to England for Jewish schooling. The next step was *aliya* and moving to Ramat Raziel in 1971. The settlement, on a back road from Beit Shemesh to Jerusalem, was founded in 1948 and named after David Raziel (1910–1941), one of the founding members of the Irgun. A major activity was agriculture, so Ben Zaken tried his hand at it, but soon he realized that his future was to be elsewhere.

Ben Zaken, with somewhat of an Italian background, decided to open an Italian restaurant in Downtown Jerusalem. His specialty was the first restaurant in Israel with fresh pasta made on the premises. As the once-restaurateur explains, there are two factors that make a memorable pasta—the species of wheat and the freshness of the product. Ben Zaken is quite clear that freshness takes precedence. The work of making pasta is not very complicated, but the process is labor-intensive. As a result, prices were higher than competition, and Ben Zaken decided to move onward to new endeavors. When asked about commercial pastas sold on supermarket shelves, Ben Zaken smiled, "They absolutely cannot compete with homemade."

On his plot of land in Ramat Raziel, Ben Zaken started growing grapes as a hobby. Even though this was not a professional effort, Ben Zaken approached his wine making with sound business sense. Even on the first run of 660 bottles of wine he affixed formal labels. "How can you give a bottle to a friend without a label?" he asked me rhetorically.

An amateurish start led to a great success. The wine he made was first-rate according to Serena Sutcliffe (born 1945), an international wine expert and Master of Wine at Sotheby's in London, who described it as "absolutely terrific ... a real *tour de force*, brilliantly made."

Why not operate an Italian restaurant with Israeli made Italian-style wines? Ben Zaken digressed, explaining that Israel has come a long way in wine production over the past twenty or so years, but quality wines must be further developed. There are wines typical of certain areas of France and Italy, but there still is not the developed taste of an "Israeli wine" *per se.* No, an Italian restaurant with a quality Italian wine list would not succeed. The market is still not ready. So, Ben Zaken gathered his two sons together, led a series of discussions, and started a family wine business, Domaine du Castel.

All of the company's grapes are grown locally in the area of Ramat Raziel, although they are originally from imported seeds. Ben Zaken attributes their quality to the climate of the Judean Hills, low humidity during the growing season, and the influence of winds coming off the Mediterranean Sea.

In 2003 a key decision was made. Domain du Castel applied for and was granted kashrut supervision. Note that *shemita* harvesting is *otzar beit din* and has Rabbanut supervision but not Beit Yosef. All products are Kosher for Passover.

The winery currently produces about one hundred thousand bottles a year. The leading variety is a Bordeaux-style red, the Grand Vin Castel. Petit Castel is a blend of the wines not used for Grand Vin Castel. Again the blend will be mainly Cabernet Sauvignon and the rest, in order of importance is Merlot, Petit Verdot, Cabernet Franc and Malbec. The wine is aged for sixteen months in French oak barrels.

One can see the barrels neatly lined up in rows in the wine cellar. For those who are curious, barrels are used no more than three times. Then they are sold to other wineries. One of the hardest jobs in the winery is to clean the barrels.

Why should one buy a Domaine du Castel wine? The average price per bottle is about 42 dollars or 32 euros but Ben Zaken stands behind the quality of the product (distributed in the UK by Kedem Wine). I found the wines to have a pleasantly smooth texture with a smooth taste on the palate. Castel is a wine to be savored and certainly not gulped down.

If you are in Israel, there is an intermediate step. In a pre-arranged visit to the winery (NIS75 person, but free with the purchase of a case of twelve bottles) you can be given a tour and explanation together with wine tasting and a sampling of *mehadrin* cheese made from goat's milk. Although wine is traditionally put into 750 milliliter bottles, each year some twenty bottles of six liters are filled with wine for use at parties.

Should you make the investment and buy Domaine du Castel wine? It is a personal decision depending upon one's financial ability. If you enjoy an excellent wine, Castel certainly qualifies. As Eli Ben Zaken jokingly says, if this is what your wife says you should bring home from the wine store, definitely do it!

Hours by arrangement. Tours in Hebrew, English and other languages available. Telephone: 02-534-2249. Wine cellar not wheelchair accessible.

Tzor'a

Teperberg Winery *(See color plates 23 & 24, p 108)*

Today the Teperberg Winery is a modern facility in Tzor'a, near Beit Shemesh, but that was not always the case. In 1870 Abraham Teperberg and his son, Ze'ev Zeid, both immigrants from Odessa, transformed a home hobby into a commercial operation and opened a winery in what is now the parking lot of the Jewish Quarter in Jerusalem's Old City. All went well until 1925, when a Mandate order prohibited "industry" in the Old City. The winery was forced to move to a location today occupied by Jerusalem's Central Bus Station. The entrance to Jerusalem was fraught with danger, particularly from the Arab villages of Lifta and Deir Yassin, so the winery moved again, to Machane Yehuda and in 1960 to a defunct winery in Motza.

Teperberg mass production means heavy investment in machinery (Sheina)

The products of the winery were more or less standard, concentrating on the sweet and rather unsophisticated wines typical of the times in Israel. In the early 1990s, however, Golan Wines revolutionized the Israeli wine market with the introduction of higher quality wines. This change was only strengthened by the advent of boutique wineries. Motti Teperberg, a fifth generation owner of the family business, made a strategic decision. He hired Shiki Rauchberger as chief winemaker, and the company shifted emphasis to high quality wines. In 2006 the Motza winery was sold off, and Teperberg wines moved to the much larger facility in Tzor'a, which was also closer to the vineyards that provide the grapes on multi-year contract.

Not only has Teperberg initiated an improvement in quality. The source of grapes has also changed. Beforehand 85 percent of the grapes that were used came from Arab growers (for the 2001 *shemita* year יבול נכרי – non-Jewish produce) and 15 percent came from Jews (not used in *shemita* and replaced in production by grapes from Cyprus). After the 2002 decision contracts were signed with more and more Jewish growers, who in recent years often grow grapes from seedlings (cuts) imported from France (with careful attention to *orla* after replanting in Israel). By the *shemita* of 2008 there was a change. Normally all wine and grape juice in the winery is under Eida supervision. For *shemita* a change was made. Grapes grown by non-Jews and imported grapes were under Eida supervison, but because of the large amount of produce from Jewish sources, Teperberg started an *otzar beit din* line with non-*mehadrin* Rabbanut Matei Yehuda supervision. For the record, after the *otzar beit din* bottling, the Eida insisted that the entire production line be *kashered.*

The wines coming out of the vineyard are of three broad qualities; the basic traditional sweet kiddush wines are the least expensive. Next is the Israeli series, medium priced and often used by catering establishments and restaurants. At the top of the list is the Teperberg series (Silver, Terra and the Premium Reserve) which were first put on the market in 2005.

Teperberg Silver wines come from grapes grown in selected vineyards in the lowlands (up to 250 meters) of the Judean Hills, such as Tzor'a. The grapes are picked each August, and the wine is ready the following July after six months of maturing in oak barrels. This contrasts with lesser quality wines, which are "young" and are available in supermarkets already in time for Passover.

The Terra wines come from wines grown at 650 meters or more, typically from the Upper Galilee, the Shomron, and the higher regions of the Judean Hills. The grapes have better aroma and color, and they mature in French oak barrels (often new barrels) for an entire year. As Shiki Rauchberger explains, choosing the right barrel is an art. A strong wine would not mature well in a three-year-old barrel; conversely, a light wine should not be matured in a new oak barrel. A house favorite is Malbec, which only recently has been produced.

Reserve wines come from selected vineyards, and about 85 percent of the production is matured for about eighteen months in barrels never used before.

Appreciating a quality wine does demand an education. Reading is one possibility, but much better is tasting, when experts are on hand to give explanations. One aspect of a wine education is to learn which wine complements the taste of which food.

In general terms red wine is often served with meat. It also complements many cheeses. White wine, on the other hand, goes well with fish. Sauvignon Blanc, for example, is a young and refreshing wine that goes well with oily fish. Riesling is better for sushi. Shiki Rauchberger has some very basic advice, "Just try different combinations."

Do you want to buy a wine barrel as a household souvenir? Teperberg, as other serious wineries, uses barrels no more than three times. Then they are sold off or discarded.

As to the kashrut of Teperberg wines, the Eida takes full responsibility, and they literally hold the keys. Their *mashgiach* opens locks even for the chief winemaker! They also approve the hiring of every worker involved with wine. All wines are labeled *mevushal* or non-*mevushal*, even though it is well known that the higher quality products (Teperberg Terra and Reserve) cannot be *mevushal* for reasons of taste. Grape juice is certainly *mevushal* according to all opinions, since it is pasteurized at 86°C (186.8°F).

Water is not added to grape juice labeled 100 percent pure. As a purchasing guideline, "Lite" wine has less alcohol content, but it can have as little as 70 percent grape. Wines, particularly in the Israeli and Teperberg lines, also have no water added.

The Teperberg Winery is not afraid of competition. They have full confidence in their wines. Boutique wineries are a factor in the market, accounting for some 20 to 25 percent of the Israeli market. Some are kosher; some are not. Some are good; some are amateurish efforts. Most are more expensive due to relatively small production. Teperberg is certainly willing to let consumers decide how their wines compare. They are the fourth largest winery in Israel, and they are looking improve their standing. From my perspective, tasting their excellent wines is a convincing experience of quality. Their Teperberg line is absolutely recommended.

Note: Tasting and purchasing on site are not possible at this time. There are plans to eventually build a visitors center.

Tzor'a Winery (See color pates 25 & 26, p 109)

The Tzor'a Winery had an interesting beginning. The late Roni James, an Egyptian-born a member of Kibbutz Tzor'a, had grown grapes for resale since the 1970s, but in 1993 the business took a significant turn. He produced his first wines in what was one of Israel's earliest boutique wineries.

The company's winemaker is Eran Pick, who learned the trade in the University of California-Davis, but the training was theoretical. He supplemented classroom experience with practical experience again in California, but also in France and Australia. In 2006 he joined the Tzor'a staff, as the winery was privatized. Today the winery's vineyards cover about 370 dunhams; half of the grapes are used by the winery, and half are sold to other wineries (both small and large).

In the 1990s the main wines were Merlot and Cabernet Sauvignon, but in 2002 when the company became kosher, Syrah was added. Other varieties of grape were planted in 2009, and in the next few years they will yield new wines. (Grapes can first be used four years after planting, and maturity begins a year or two afterwards.) As Pick explains, 95 percent of the work involved in making wine is in the vineyard.

Supervision of the company's 80,000 bottles each year is by the U.S. O-K Laboratories and Rabbanut Matei Yehudah, yet a vast percentage of sales is to non-kosher restaurants in the Tel Aviv area! Kosher is out of principle and not because of market demand. The same is true in New York; although Tzor'a Wine is available in the "Israeli Section" of wine stores, it is more often to be found in restaurants (and not necessarily kosher ones). Restaurants are a big market with some selling between three and four hundred bottles of Tzor'a wines per month. Pick estimates that 75 percent of boutique wine is sold by restaurants.

In the last *shemita* year *heter mechira* (Jewish land "sold" to a non-Jew) was used (not approved by O-K), but there were restrictions. Selection of grapes was problematic, and clusters had to be torn from the vine rather than cut with scissors. Nor could this wine be exported to kosher markets.

Harvesting is always done by hand, and at night to protect the picked grapes from the day's heat. The grapes are then selected twice, first by cluster, then by individual grape. Labeling with Tzor'a is unique, with wines being called after the vineyard in which the grapes are grown. The entry level, Judean Hills, contains wine from red grapes grown in the Shoresh and Neve Ilan vineyards. The next in quality is a white wine, Neve Ilan, coming only from that vineyard; Shoresh has both red and white. The top of the line is Misty Hills (Cabernet Sauvignon and Syrah blended together), of which only three thousand bottles are made each year.

Visits to the winery are encouraged. The winery is open Sunday–Thursday 1000–1700, Friday 1000–1400. During these hours visitors can hear about the company, taste wines, and even eat a bit of cheese. Fee: NIS25, refundable with a wine purchase. It is recommended that the visitor or the winery *mashgiach* open all bottles of wine. Workshops can be arranged by telephone as well as trips to the vineyards. To reach the winery, drive from the Jerusalem–Tel Aviv Highway south on Route 38. Turn right into Tzor'a two kilometers after the railroad tracks, then follow the signs (to the right of the Tzor'a center).

Mony Winery *(See color plates 27 & 28, p 110)*

There are numerous cases of Jewish–Arab cooperation, particularly in the commercial sector. The winery just outside Tzor'a is one example.

Shakeeb Artul, a Christian Arab from the Galilee had a family tradition of growing olives and grapes. On one trip to central Israel in the 1980s he decided to lease a large plot of land from a monastery near

Mony's Vineyards

Tzor'a in the Beit Shemesh region. The monastery had produced wine for sacramental purposes, so the land looked promising. After not too long a time wine was produced, and even the monastery stopped its own wine making and started to buy from Artul. There was, however, one significant glitch. There is only a limited market for non-kosher wine, so a commercial decision was made. The company contracted for rabbinic supervision, and kosher wine was made.

Why the name "Mony?" This is a family business. One son is in charge of the winery, another is responsible for the vineyards, and another deals with olives and olive oil. There was, however, a fourth son. Mony was his Arabic name; he unfortunately passed away in the 1990s. As Shakeeb explains, naming the wine "Mony" is his way of always remembering his son. So, the company not only produces kosher wine, but even calls it by an Arabic name!

If you are dubious about the kashrut, a discussion with the rabbinic supervisor will quickly allay all of your fears. He assures that the only keys are held by him and by his assistant. Supervision is also given in the names of the Beit Yosef, the American O-K Laboratories and the local Rabbinical Council. The supervision is also backed up by cameras (not a replacement for human presence, but an additional measure to record all actions). *Shemita*, for example, is not a problem of *heter mechira*, since the land is clearly owned by non-Jews. There is also absolutely no water added to any of the wines. (Note that the tasting room is not under supervision, since there is no control over who serves the wine. In the company store there are wines for sale, clearly marked "non-kosher," that were produced before rabbinic supervision was introduced).

Very often the chief winemaker is schooled in the art of making wine with wide experience in French and/or Italian wineries, but again Mony is different. Samuel Soroka, originally from Montréal, has his academic background in anthropology and photography, then food chemistry. Wine quickly took his fancy as he read professional food publications. He accrued experience with wine in the Napa Valley, California, and not in France, but in Australia and in Israel (with Carmel where he started their boutique line). As he explains, Australia is less restrictive than traditional Europe and allows more innovation in winemaking. Australian wines are mixed according to taste, and preset rules do not dictate acidity or the type of oak in the barrels used for aging (if oak is chosen altogether). He came to Mony in 2009.

From a marketing point of view Mony is unique from several perspectives. They make numerous types of wine, but they are limited to a production of about eighty thousand bottles per year. Excess grapes, all grown in the family's vineyards, are sold to other wineries. The company also makes "wine to order." There is, for example, a large American wine importer who orders ten thousand bottles at a time of a slightly sweeter Rosé.

Unlike many boutique wineries, Mony picks grapes by machine and not by hand, thus keeping the price down (a saving passed on to the consumer). According to Soroka, this allows quick picking at night, protecting the grapes from influence by daylight heat or long storage in the field after harvesting. The entire process is accompanied by a *mashgiach*.

What constitutes a fine wine? The Mony philosophy is not only taste, which obviously plays a primary role. According to the company owner, the price must be commensurate with quality. Wines at outlandish prices very rarely are of equivalent superb quality.

Mony wines are found in stores, but a significant part of sales are to restaurants and large wine businesses both in Israel and abroad. If you are looking for an intriguing experience, perhaps the best way to buy Mony wine is to visit the company store at the winery. There the entire line of Mony wines is for sale at extremely reasonable prices. And, do not overlook the olives (also kosher)!

This writer's evaluation: Very good wines at an extremely fair price, and warm hospitality that will be long remembered. Well worth a visit (and a taste). Telephone: 02-991-6629.

Tzuba

The Kibbutz started planting grapes for the wholesale market in 1996, but several years later a marketing decision was made. They would make their own wine in addition to selling grapes to others. First production was in 2005 under the profession guidance of winemaker Paul Dubb of South African background. By 2011 the winery was marketing seventy thousand bottles per year.

There are basically eight varieties of wine, some of which are blends. One that is not blended is a 100 percent Chardonnay (half aged six months in first-time use French oak barrels, half aged in stainless steel, then mixed). Dubb's philosophy is to use the best grapes possible, but not to compete with French wines. In reds, Pinot Noir is a pride of the house. The premium wine is Metzuda, based on Cabernet. Tzuba wine is made to stress the excellent growing conditions of the Judean Hills. The wines are based upon a 450 dunham vineyard owned by the kibbutz.

Kosher supervision is the O-K from the United States and also from the Matei Yehudah Rabbinate. Twenty percent of the wine is exported to the United States; thirty percent is sold at the winery.

The winery is open daily 0800 until 1600 for explanations and wine tasting. Arrangements can be made in advance for the rabbinic supervisor to open bottles and pour the wine. There is a NIS25 per person fee, including a visit to the ancient wine press. Although individual and family visits need not be coordinated, advance notice is always best. Visitors can be received in both Hebrew and English. Telephone: 02-534-7678.

The winery has another unrelated product. Bring your own bottle, and fill it up! The charge is NIS35 per liter.

To the North

Anatot Winery

Two Israelis, Aharon Helfgott (founder of modern Anatot) and Arnon Erez each had a similar hobby—to make wine. In 1998 they joined forces, took serious courses in wine production, and started the Anatot Winery. As Erez explains, his instructor at Hebrew University told him he might as well throw out all of his amateurish production.

A regular office printer makes the wine bottle labels

Today Anatot produces only some ten thousand bottles of red wine per year, a very small quantity even for a boutique winery. Since production is low, the winery still has not lost the personal touch of the two owners. They are the only workers! And much of the equipment was produced by them. Helfgott is the electrician, and Erez is the mechanic. Together they made a wine press from a tractor motor and scrap metal, some of which came from a building site. Keep the costs down! Standard office equipment was redesigned to paste labels on bottles; the labels are ordered from the printer with a space between pairs, so that one can be applied to the front of the bottle and the other to the back. At the beginning even the wine barrels were bought second-hand from a major Israeli winery, then totally refurbished.

This is a homespun industry in every sense. The winery is under the steps and in the backyard to Helfgott's home.

The visitor will certainly be impressed by the ingenuity involved in setting up this winery, but words of *halachic* caution must be added. The grapes are from a religious vineyard where *terumah* and *ma'aser* are taken, and there is no *shemita* crop. The wine itself, however, has *no* rabbinic supervision due to Sabbath observance problems. This winery is included to illustrate the pure ingenuity in wine production. It is absolutely unique!

Beit El

When visiting Beit El do not neglect the Beit El Winery, where Hillel Manne has brought his California know-how to produce Merlot and Cabernet Sauvignon wines since 2002. The boutique winery produces about eight thousand bottles per year, with plans to expand production. Visits to the winery can be arranged by calling 054-524-0936.

Har Bracha (Mount Blessing)

Grapes were first planted in 1998 for the small winery 840 meters above sea level on the slopes of Mount Grizim in Northern Samaria with the aim of selling grapes to other wineries. History, though, took a turn. The first commercial vintage for wine production in-house was in 2007 by owner Nir Lavi. The house specialty is a variety of red wines including blends. One of the house specialties is a port wine aged twenty-four months in French oak barrels.

Visits can be arranged by calling 052-577-5156.

P'sagot *(See color plate 29, p 111)*

In 1998 Meir Berg and his family planted the first Cabernet Sauvignon grapes for wine production, which began in 2002. Today P'sagot vineyards cover forty dunhams. The winery produces Cabernet Sauvignon, Merlot, Chardonnay, and Viognier wines as well as a Prat port-style wine (a fortified wine historically originating in the Douro Valley in Portugal). Prat won a gold medal in the 2006 Terravino competition, though in 2010 winery owners decided not to participate in the competition. Instead they are setting their sights on more competitive European events. A contributing factor is that most of the one hundred thousand annual bottle production of P'sagot wine is sold abroad.

The winery's premier product and winner of a least eight awards is Edom 2006, a blend of Cabernet Sauvignon (40 percent), Merlot (5 percent), Cabernet Franc (10 percent), and Petite Verdot (5 percent). The wine is carefully aged in oak barrels for eighteen months. It is usually sold in Israeli retail outlets for between NIS110 and NIS130 per bottle (NIS110 in the visitors' center where a full selection of P'sagot wines can be purchased).

A visit to the P'sagot winery is a very positive experience. Not only is there the winery (the most organized in the Jerusalem area for tourists to visit); there is also an entire visitors center including guided tour

P'sagot Winery storage room. Tours of the winery are available (Sheina)

of wine making with an explicative movie, an audio visual presentation, and a restaurant (under *mehadrin* rabbinic supervision) for a light meal or snack, and wine tasting.

The audio visual presentation is interactive in a choice of Hebrew, English or French, and provides an excellent introduction to Israeli issues of security, geography and demography. The presentation can be adjusted to length according to the tourist's time available. Its flexible design also permits use either as a straight learning experience or as a competitive quiz.

Particularly during Chol HaMoed there are festive activities including camel riding. Prior reservations at 02-997-9333 are necessary. The price of visits ranges from NIS25 for a tour to NIS125 for a tour, wine tasting, and a gourmet meal. (Note: The Visitors' Center is sometimes rented out for affairs. When outside catering is used, the exact kashrut certification should be verified.) Plan on two hours for a visit plus extra time for any dining.

Ofra

Domaine Ventura from Ofra produces a gold prize winning Gran Vin Cabernet Sauvignon 2005. A single bottle is priced in the $85–$120 class. Another Gold Medal winner and slightly less expensive ($50–$80) is Gran Vin Rubens 2005, produced by the same company. One should not be intimidated by these prices. All of the company's wines have won medals, but the vast majority is sold at much lower prices.

David Ventura, an immigrant from France, who takes pride in producing a superior French-style wine, is the company founder and owner. He is religiously observant, and has arranged that his wines are produced with the kashrut supervision of the local rabbinate, the O-U, and Beit Yosef. The first harvests for Ventura were in 2006 and 2007, but in 2008 there was no wine produced. Why? *Shemita,* of course.

Visits to the winery are always welcome, but prior arrangement is necessary. If Domaine Ventura is not as commercialized as P'sagot, Ventura makes up for this by his personal warmth and hospitality. Explanations about the company's wines are in Hebrew or French.

Ventura wines are coming down in price as production increases and export expands to the United States, France, and Italy.

Rechalim

The Erez Winery was founded in 2003 by Erez Sadon, and later it was renamed the Tura Winery. Production is now more than 10,000 bottles per year (all under O-U and local rabbinate certification), most of which is Cabernet Sauvignon, Merlot and Chardonnay. There is a Port with 20 percent alcohol, aged twenty-four months in French barrels, then another year in bottles. The winery has also entered the olive oil business, and it producers another unusual product—apple cider with 5.7 percent alcohol.

Visitors are welcome, but there is a NIS25 fee to cover tasting. To arrange a visit call 052-312-8000.

Shilo

Mayer Chomer, born and raised in Mexico, always had a dream of opening a winery even though by education he is a former yeshiva student and a lawyer with a Ph.D. in Criminal Law. His story is that of a dream come true. As Chomer explains, "I am an idealist, but a very pragmatic idealist." He decided the time was ripe to act, but where should he start his winery? Chomer recalled the Biblical vision of vineyards in the Shomron, "After doing some technical and professional research, I was convinced that the Shomron is by far the best terrain in Israel for wine." He started his winery in Shilo in 2005. Today Shilo is another of the relatively new boutique wineries that have sprung up in Israel since the late 1990s.

At the Shilo Winery

Primary products are Merlot, Shiraz, Chardonnay, Sauvignon and Rosé. A unique product is Mosaic 2006, a robust blend of Merlot (60 percent), Cabernet Franc (20 percent), Cabernet Sauvignon (7 percent), Petit Verdot (7 percent), and Syrah (6 percent). All wines are not *mevushal* and are under the kashrut supervision of the O-K, Chatam Sofer-Bnei Braq, and Rabbanut Matei Binyamin.

Tours by appointment. Telephone: 02-990-0736.

Note

Every effort has been made to provide accurate information, but there will probably be changes, additions, and deletions. For updates the reader can access the following link: http://thekeypublish.com/index.php/vmchk/Jewish-Journeys-Near-Jerusalem.html

1 kilometer	×	0.6213 miles
1 meter	×	3.2808 feet
1 dunham	×	0.24710 acres
1 hectare	×	10 000 m^2

Index

DATE			